The young hero

in American fiction

The young hero
in American fiction

A motif for teaching literature

by

F. ANTHONY DE JOVINE

OHIO UNIVERSITY

APPLETON-CENTURY-CROFTS
EDUCATIONAL DIVISION
MEREDITH CORPORATION

New York

PRINTED IN THE UNITED STATES OF AMERICA

390-26013-4

To my mother and father

Contents

	Page
Preface	ix
Introduction	1

The Teaching of Content

| 1. Characterization | 11 |
| 2. Theme | 46 |

The Teaching of Style

3. Symbolism as style	69
4. Irony and paradox as style	88
5. Romanticism and realism as style	107
6. Tragedy and comedy as style	121
7. Structure as style	136
Conclusion	153
Bibliography	161
Index of fictional works	169
Index of principal fictional characters	171

Preface

This book is based on the premise that one cannot discuss the teaching of fiction without discussing fiction. In deciding what constitutes a suitable body of fiction for discussion however, one encounters a number of difficulties in making selections which are suitable for inclusion in a syllabus that is comprehensive, unified, and pedagogically viable. Works of American literature in which the hero is a young person have been chosen for this discussion for reasons which minimize these difficulties. Many of these works are acknowledged masterpieces of world literature and are typically included in courses in American literature in both college and high school. They often focus on similar themes, but at the same time illustrate diverse styles of fictional art. Finally, the problems and situations dramatized in these works relate directly to those which have perenially confronted youth in all civilized cultures in their dealings with adults and their search for identity and fulfillment.

In order to keep this book a reasonable length it was necessary to be strict in making choices. Nevertheless, there is enough material here for the teacher to construct a study unit which can cover an entire school year. Those teachers who would want to replace or supplement some of these works are urged to consult W. Tasker Witham's *The Adolescent in the American Novel*, 1920–1960 (New York: Frederick Ungar Publishing Co., 1964), an exhaustive and comprehensive study which lists, describes, and analyzes hundreds of novels written over a forty-year span, and which contains a superb system of cross-reference with which the teacher can pinpoint works dealing with specific problems of adolescents in regard to sex, family, school, vocation, society, and related areas.

In this book primary consideration will be given to four works: *Billy Budd, The Catcher in The Rye, The Adventures of Huckleberry Finn,* and *The Red Badge of Courage.* Secondary consideration will be given to a number of other works: *The Adventures of Augie March, An American Tragedy, Intruder in the Dust, Look Homeward, Angel, Martin Eden, On the Road, Other Voices, Other Rooms, Redburn, The Red Pony, A Separate Peace, Studs Lonigan, This Side of Paradise, Winesburg, Ohio* and selected short stories of Aiken, Cather, Faulkner, Hawthorne, Hemingway, and Trilling. Occasionally, reference will be made to works not involving the young hero in order to clarify a point or to advance an argument.

These works share a central hero or protagonist who undergoes a process of initiation which results either in desirable personal growth, or, in some cases, in deterioration of character. They also share the fact that, with a minimum of teacher help, they are understandable to the student in varying degrees. Of course, some are more readily understandable than others. *Martin Eden* reads more easily than *Billy Budd* or *Intruder in the Dust.* Faulkner's short version of "The Bear" is far more readable and less complex than the longer version. Indeed, the latter is suited to only the most able student. A work like *An American Tragedy* requires less teacher help than one like *The Catcher in the Rye* for the student to achieve proper appreciation of these works.

No lesson plans as such will be included in this book. The commentary, together with passages from literary critics and authorities on the teaching of English, will contain built-in suggestions to aid the teacher in constructing projects for classroom activities.

Some teachers will probably have no immediate occasion to teach courses in American literature which would include some of the works discussed here. This book can still be of value, however, in helping to formulate principles and approaches that can apply to fictional works not in American literature.

Although this book addresses itself primarily to the secondary teacher, its materials are suitable also for introductory literature courses at the college level.

F. A. D.

The young hero

in American fiction

Introduction

All art consists of two basic components—content and style. Synonyms for these terms may be such pairs as substance and technique, matter and manner, or, in terms easily understood by students, the *what* and the *how* of a work. The term *form* is partially synonomous with style. More accurately, it is the end result of the style employed by the artist. The teacher must use every resource at his command to develop in the student the ability to comprehend, in as detailed a manner as the student's capacities will permit, just what an author has accomplished, the ability to identify the alternatives the author has at his disposal in accomplishing his task, and finally, and most importantly, the ability to pass judgment on the author's total effort, based on the evidence gleaned from a careful study of the text. In short, the student undertakes a process of analysis—the dismantling of a fictional work—in order to achieve a meaningful synthesis. This process of analysis and synthesis is the activity of literary criticism, and the student must be disabused early of the stereotyped notion that the word *criticism* implies a derogatory statement about a work. The process of criticism does require an initial act of destruction (analysis) but this is done in order to achieve an original re-creation (synthesis). Analysis is often done arbitrarily and by trial and error. And, one may begin to analyze at

1

any point in the work. Synthesis requires a more orderly and rational procedure of reconstruction, however, which at its best leads to an original discovery or unique insight. One can observe this process in its most elemental form during a spontaneous classroom discussion. Students usually enter such discussions with vague and impressionistic attitudes toward a work; then, after a free give and take of ideas involving both the teacher and the student, the student (as well as the teacher who learns through teaching) comes to some definite and verifiable conclusions—the verification here being based on the data contained within the text of the work. Often, as will be demonstrated later, there may be disagreements over the validity of conclusions derived from divergent insights. This often argues a case, however, for the rich possibilities of the analysis-synthesis approach in assisting the student to develop a heightened sense of appreciation, and an intellectual awareness of the complexity of fictional art.

All this by no means is intended to suggest that all critical conclusions are valid merely because they have been arrived at by analysis and synthesis. However, when the student does begin to acquire a proficiency in the use of sound critical techniques through the proper use of analysis and synthesis, he also begins to experience the aesthetic delights of being a co-creator of sorts of the work under study, and in this sense has as much at stake in the work as the author himself—especially if the student can be shown, as is often the case, that authors themselves experience difficulty in interpreting their own works. Browning, Joyce, Frost, and Faulkner in varying degrees provide cases in point. It seems most certain that Twain would be unable to write the kind of criticism which has appeared in the last generation on *The Adventures of Huckleberry Finn.* He tells us as much in his humorous preface:

Persons attempting to find a motive in this narrative will be prosecuted; persons attempting to find a moral in it will be banished; and persons attempting to find a plot in it will be shot.

Certainly Mark Twain wrote this with tongue in cheek, but its prophetic implications resound in high irony. Melville, too, might be puzzled over what has been gleaned from his works in recent years. Henry James is probably an exception to the foregoing generalization. The prefaces to his works reveal a keen awareness of what he was about in his work. The student must see that once a work is published it is in the public domain and is fair game for interpretation by everyone from elementary school to graduate school. And it is for this reason that the teacher's role is crucial in teaching the techniques of intelligent interpretation.

There is a danger in one's taking the analysis-synthesis system of pedagogy too literally, of committing the error of the "reductive fallacy" which, John Dewey tells us,

results from an oversimplification. It exists when some constituent of the work of art is isolated and then the whole is reduced to terms of this single isolated element. . . . The same principle applies when technique is taken apart from its connection with form.[1]

Thus, one cannot set up content and style as mutually exclusive categories. G. W. Stone illustrates Dewey's point with a cogent, specific example in his statement on romanticism and realism:

When we use the word romanticism to place a work or a writer in a formal category, as though we had thereby settled an issue, arrived at a conclusion, or disposed of a case, we simply dismiss all the interesting and important problems. A useful definition of the term romantic does not establish an unequivocal category. . . . The meaning of the word will change in almost every context.

Thus, too, in the same place does Stone deal with the term "realistic," which

refers not to an absolute but to a relative determination of certain qualities. A work is more or less realistic than some other work.[2]

In a more practical vein, George Sampson anticipates the difficulties a teacher may have with a student in trying to instill in him an analytic attitude. Few students submit readily to the tasks of analysis. They would rather read for "fun," little realizing that critical analysis properly applied leads to a type of high pleasure which transcends mere "fun." Taking an example from the discipline of music appreciation, Sampson asks:

What pleasure should we get from a performance of the C minor symphony if the conductor stopped the orchestra at every occurrence of the main theme

[1] John Dewey, *Art as Experience* (New York: Putnam, 1958), p. 315.
[2] George Winchester Stone, ed., *Issues, Problems, and Approaches in the Teaching of English* (New York: Holt, Rinehart and Winston, 1963), p. 62.

to expatiate upon the wonderful significance with which Beethoven can invest a simple rhythmic phrase . . .?[3]

This statement suggests that analysis can be a matter of mere picking apart, destroying the continuity and flow so necessary to good art. The statement does not consider, however, the process of synthesis which reconstructs the work into a more meaningful unit when re-experienced. The student ought to submit to the admittedly artificial and laborious process of analysis early in his education to enable him to develop critical judgment. He submits to a similar process when he learns how to walk, talk, read, write, or drive a car. As his critical tastes become more refined, however, so, too, do his skills of analysis, which become almost an art unto themselves. Analysis ought to be something more than an awkward, unrewarding, unnatural process of picking apart. In time it should become an instrument at the student's disposal, which he uses adeptly, unselfconsciously, and at best even intuitively to attain a higher end—an insight into a reality otherwise unattainable, a confrontation with a unique truth that only the artist has the talent to create, but which the student must earn by applying his intellect energetically and correctly to the work. The sooner the secondary school student masters this application, the better are his chances for making his college experiences more meaningful. Or, if he is not college bound, the better are his chances for enlarging his enjoyment of life through the leisure that our society is supplying in ever-increasing abundance.

The distinction between content and style is an artificial one which the teacher must employ only because few human minds can comprehend an artistic entity, or any other complex pattern, instantaneously. In a sense the human mind is like a data-processing machine. It selects, classifies, and organizes raw data into a meaningful whole. The quality of this whole depends upon the type of mind which is processing the data, and upon the techniques employed by the teacher in assisting the student to process it so that the final result, the basic unity of content and style, can be realized. The success of this activity need not require that the teacher have a finer mind than the student, but he should have more experience and sophistication in the use of critical techniques, and the ability to tap fully the intellectual capacities of the student.

[3] George Sampson, *English for the English* (London: Cambridge, 1921), in J. N. Hook, *The Teaching of High School English* (New York: Ronald, 1965), p. 211.

One can state axiomatically that content is style and style is content, while yet having to concede to the paradox that they are distinctly separate entities. Henry James reveals this insight when he states:

The idea and the form are the needle and the thread, and I never heard of a guild of tailors who recommended the use of the thread without the needle, or the needle without the thread.[4]

Mark Schorer seems to say that it is impossible to have good content with poor style and poor content with good style:

The difference between content, or experience, and achieved content, or art, is technique. . . . Technique alone objectifies the materials of art; hence technique alone evaluates those materials.[5]

John Dewey in effect joins the two concepts in an interdependent relationship:

Yet the act itself is exactly *what* it is because of *how* it is done. In the act there is no distinction, but perfect integration of manner and content, form and substance. . . . Means and ends coalesce. If we run over in mind a number of such cases we quickly see that all the cases in which means and ends are external to one another are non-esthetic.[6]

George H. Henry offers an insight that goes beyond a mere marriage of content and style:

There isn't a humanist who does not harp upon the interplay of form and content in a work of art. John Ciardi some time ago went so far as to speak of 'form as a kind of experience that goes most deeply into whatever a man is: Dance, ritual, religious ceremony, political ceremony, or poetic encounter. . . .' Implied in the relation of form and substance is the deeper one of life and art which, at bottom, is man's innate desire to impress a world, an order, upon the miscellaneous array of sensations and happenings that flood upon him every waking moment year in and year out. This union of form and substance becomes an experience.[7]

[4] Henry James, *The Art of Fiction and Other Essays* (New York: Oxford, 1948), p. 18.

[5] Mark Schorer, "Technique as Discovery," *Hudson Review*, I (Spring, 1948), in John W. Aldridge, ed., *Critiques and Essays in Modern Fiction*, 1920–1951 (New York: Ronald, 1952), pp. 67, 71.

[6] Dewey, pp. 109, 198.

[7] George H. Henry, "Method: The New Home of the Liberal Spirit," in Dwight L. Burton, ed., *English Education Today* (Champaign: National Council of Teachers of English, 1963), p. 19.

Nevertheless, despite this consensus on the inseparability of content and style, and on their equality of rank in the total scheme of art, teachers tend to put more emphasis on the former than the latter. B. Bernard Cohen states clearly that,

The word *form* means the shape any literary work assumes as a result of all the technical resources employed by an author. Content is the material—ideas, emotions, events, people—which the author is shaping. A fusion of form and content occurs when the author has chosen and successfully employed the most suitable technical devices to develop his subject matter. Since it is often easier to talk about an author's ideas, the emphasis in literary analysis is too frequently placed upon content.[8]

One encounters the same difficulty in teaching composition. It is easier to discuss ideas and their implications than to demonstrate to students how an author dramatizes and makes viable his ideas through the particular way in which he communicates them. And, in taking this path of least resistance, we do the student a great disservice by making him insensitive to the subtleties of style.

Essentially, style is a more elusive concept to grasp than content. It is easier to recognize than explain. Perhaps a good guideline, reduced to simplistic terms, which may assist the teacher in making students more sensitive to the subtleties of style, lies in Mark Schorer's phrase "achieved content." We know intuitively whether a fictional work is good, poor, or mediocre. If it is good we experience from it, according to our tastes and our capacities for discrimination, certain delight; if it is poor we do not. It is more difficult, however, to say why we react as we do. But if it is the *how* that achieves, influences, or determines the *what*, then through the *how* we can better appreciate the *what*, and through the *what* we can better appreciate the *how*—the one without the other being but a vacuous conception. Both *The Adventures of Huckleberry Finn* and *Uncle Tom's Cabin* make powerful statements on the evils of slavery. In the former, however, the statement is demonstrated or "achieved," while in the latter it is merely presented. To be able to understand *why* we make this judgment constitutes a first step in unlocking the secrets of style.

All that has been said thus far in regard to content and style in art applies equally to the controversy between colleges of arts and sciences and colleges of education over the relative merits of content

[8] B. Bernard Cohen, *Writing About Literature* (Chicago: Scott, Foresman, 1963), p. 23.

and method in teaching. One could argue that like content and style in art, content and method in teaching are necessary to each other and inseparable. A can-opener needs a can and vice versa. One too often hears of the teacher "who knows his stuff but can't put it across in class." One knows of the well-constructed lesson plan, worked out with precise logic, adhering faithfully to the time-honored pedagogical formula of objective, presentation, and evaluation, and yet proving a useless tool in the hands of a teacher who cannot generate a learning situation. Teaching is a conscious process. True, there are elusive elements in it as there are in art. In all good teaching, however, there is a method. It may not be so obvious as the content presented, but it is there, nonetheless, as is style in an accomplished work of art.

Dwight L. Burton, in paraphrasing Edward J. Gordon, has stated:

In working out questions for writing about or discussing a piece of literature Edward J. Gordon has identified five levels, from simplest to most difficult, according to the ability each level demands: to remember a fact; to prove a generalization that sombody else has made; to make one's own generalization; to generalize from a book to its application in life; and to carry over the generalization into one's own behavior.[9]

If, as here suggested, the intelligent, systematic study of literature can lead to an improvement in human behavior, then, indeed, the teacher has a unique opportunity to contribute toward attaining this end, despite the fact that much of human history sadly illustrates that such an attainment is often at best a quixotic ideal, a consummation more devoutly to be wished for than realized, but nonetheless to be striven for.

[9] Dwight L. Burton, *Literature Study in the High Schools* (New York: Holt, Rinehart and Winston, 1964), p. 275.

The teaching of content

1

Characterization

In his preface to *Look Homeward, Angel*, Thomas Wolfe states, "We are the sum of all the moments of our lives." In this statement he gets to the essence of what a person really is, and suggests a good working definition of the concept of characterization. But, like all simplistic definitions, it is only a starting point; it establishes, so to speak, a beachhead, and requires careful elaboration if it is to become anything more than a sweeping generalization which can do little to add to the student's ability to comprehend the meaning of character.

B. Bernard Cohen suggests a nine-point approach through which these "moments" can be examined in detail, and their "sum" viewed as a meaningful whole. Cohen's approach to the interpretation of character is presented in the following guidelines, somewhat modified for the purposes of this discussion:

1. Determine whether the character's description gives any clues to his personality.

2. Study his actions and words to see if they have any bearing on his character.

3. Examine his conscious and subconscious thought processes.

4. Clarify his motivations.

5. Note carefully his responses and attitudes towards other people and ideas.

6. Consider him in the light of what others say of him.

7. Establish adequate justification for any change in his character.

8. Try to determine what the author's attitude is toward him.

9. Compare and contrast him with other characters.[1]

[1] Cohen, pp. 114–15.

These are excellent guidelines for the teacher to use to assist the student to move beyond simple generalization. Point nine is perhaps the most useful because if used as a main guideline it will tend naturally to encompass the remaining points. In this chapter the technique of comparison and contrast will be employed at various times in an attempt to develop a way to facilitate the teaching of characterization.

In interpreting character, the student gains a sort of omniscience, which gives him the power to look directly into the soul of another. This privileged position, if properly used and appreciated by the reader, can lead to vicarious delights which most people cannot find enough first-hand experiences to fulfill. T. S. Eliot in a famous statement has justified the reading of fiction on the grounds that it is impossible for us in a typical lifetime to know enough people, and to know them well, objectively, and in depth. Good fiction serves to correct this deficiency to an extent, and thus the artist performs a valuable social function by making it possible through the medium of words for us to compensate for the limitations imposed by the short span of a lifetime—provided that we are willing to make use of his talent by applying our analytical skills to his work.

The professional critic has done much to classify characters according to personality type, and to analyze them according to their complexity of behavior and attitude. Much of this criticism can be of great value to the teacher in assisting him to teach the concept of characterization. The student must learn to distinguish between a character who may be either a good or bad person, or a composite of these qualities, and a character who is *convincingly* a good or bad person. This poses an aesthetic judgment as well as a moral one. The convincing or well-created character, whether a good or a bad person, must have a moral quality that is complex (and is not easy to understand without the exertion of intellectual effort.) Only the artist with special insight and a unique talent to express that insight can create such a character. In F. Scott Fitzgerald's *This Side of Paradise*, Father D'Arcy makes this point clear to young Amory Blaine in his letter which distinguishes between the character who is a "personality" and the character who is a "personage"—the former signifying vitality and perceptiveness, the latter, insipidity and dullness of person.[2]

[2] F. Scott Fitzgerald, *This Side of Paradise* (New York: Dell, 1948), p. 109.

E. M. Forster, in his *Aspects of the Novel*, which is somewhat out-dated but by no means obsolete or unreadable, offers some excellent insights into the interpretation of character which can be of great value to the student. Starting with the premise that "it is the function of the novelist to reveal the hidden life at its source,"[3] he goes on to develop a nomenclature through which the student can acquire a sensitivity to the nuances of characterization. Forster assigns characters to two classes—flat and round. Flat characters are types, "constructed round a single idea or quality. [But] When there is more than one factor in them we get the beginning of the curve towards the round."[4] Flat characters "can be expressed in a single sentence, . . . they . . . [are] not changed by circumstances; they . . . [move] through circumstances."[5]

To Loban, "Poor fiction depends upon stock characters and situations, stale humor, prefabricated phrases, and static characterization. In fiction of merit . . . characters grow and change."[6] Perhaps the word "change" could be replaced by the word "develop," which would more accurately suggest a series of organic changes taking place within the character and modifying his personality by degrees. Character growth is an organic development, not a mere process of mechanistic change. And this development occurs most dramatically, convincingly, and impressively when the character in question is under stress and faces a crisis situation, as does a truly round character when confronted with conflicting alternatives or ambivalences imposed from within or without. Unlike the flat character, his responses are neither easily predictable nor susceptible to simple analysis, though some type of analysis must be attempted by the student. It is the author's responsibility to assist the reader in tracing the development of character by putting into the work built-in insights and clues which serve as markers in the exposition of the story. The author can do only part of the job, however. The student must do, or better yet, earn the rest. Thurston touches on this problem in his observation that,

[3] E. M. Forster, *Aspects of the Novel* (New York: Harcourt, Brace & World, 1954) p. 45.

[4] *Ibid.*, p. 67.

[5] *Ibid.*, pp. 68–69.

[6] Walter Loban *et al.*, *Teaching Language and Literature, Grades* 7–12 (New York: Harcourt, Brace & World, 1961), p. 258.

Any intelligent reader has a very reasonable skepticism about sudden spiritual or moral change. The author must prove to him that the character was well on the way toward the change before it actually takes place, and doing this takes up most of the author's story.[7]

Bergson defines the flat character type as

the man who will listen to nothing to the man who will see nothing, and from this latter to the one who sees only what he wants to see. A stubborn spirit ends by adjusting things to its own way of thinking, instead of accommodating its thoughts to things.[8]

To Bergson the flat character is monstrously ludicrous, utterly selfish, and ridiculously unconscious: "Any individual is comic who automatically goes his own way without troubling himself about getting into touch with the rest of his fellow beings . . . we are never ridiculous except in some point that remains hidden from our own consciousness."[9] Burton distinguishes between round and flat characters through his question: "Does the author make us feel *with* the characters or only about them?"[10] His variant terms for round and flat are the archetypal, a comprehensive character who has inherited and reflects the universal experience of the human race as represented in Jung's concept of "the collective consciousness" of man, and the stereotypal who "lacks individuality and is based not on racial experience but on oversimplification and half truths."[11]

The truly round character is an imaginative person who accepts chaos and disorder as a challenge, and through magnificent acts of will which often entail great risks and uncertain ventures into the unknown, tries to impose order on and extract meaning from the confusion about him. The young student must learn to become a round person in his own right. Margaret Mead observes that "The principal causes of our adolescent's difficulty are the presence of conflicting standards and the

[7] Jarvis A. Thurston, ed., *Reading Modern Short Stories* (Chicago: Scott, Foresman, 1955), p. 9.
[8] Henri Bergson, "Laughter," in Wylie Sypher, *Comedy* (Garden City: Doubleday, 1956), p. 180.
[9] *Ibid.*, pp. 147, 169.
[10] Burton, p. 93.
[11] *Ibid.*, p. 149.

belief that every individual should make his or her own choice."[12] And the determination of this "choice" really means, as Heraclitus puts it, that a man's character and his destiny are inextricably interlocked.[13] The process by which a man moves from what he was to what he is to what he probably will be constitutes the continuum on which his character develops, and involves the Aristotelian notion of becoming (the round character) as against the Platonic notion of merely being (the flat character). Good fiction illustrates convincingly that within certain bounds a man can affect his own destiny, that what he is stems from what he was, and that his present state of being is usually crucial in influencing the courses of action he chooses which ultimately determine his destiny. Thus, one could argue that the young student who undertakes to study literature seriously can acquire the kinds of insight which can help him to develop patterns of behavior that, hopefully, can shape his destiny in a proper manner. At least this ought to be one norm that guides the teacher in the preparation and presentation of his lessons. But the teacher must do this subtly and indirectly, for students ordinarily object to studying literature for overtly didactic purposes. Nevertheless, students are much more sensitive to the problems of morality than they are commonly given credit for, and in a spirited discussion they do not hesitate to make moral judgments on the actions of characters or the intentions of an author, if such intentions are apparent, as they usually are in some degree. But, usually, the more "moral" an author's intention, the greater the likelihood that his art will suffer as a result. Again, Harriet Beecher Stowe and Mark Twain provide cases in point.

It is the author's job to create an aesthetically convincing work for the student-reader, who then proceeds to interpret the work in the light of his own experiences and with a perception that is directly proportional to his talents. The teacher serves as middleman in this process, just as the professional critic serves as middleman between author and teacher in providing the wherewithal which is in turn modified and presented to the students. This is most necessary when the works under study are complex and difficult for the common reader to understand and appreciate. The central works of this discussion involve varying degrees and kinds of complexity and difficulty. Fortunately, many able critics have done much to illuminate some of these problems. In this

[12] Margaret Mead, in Loban, p. 601, in Mead's *Coming of Age*, p. 154.
[13] S. H. Butcher, *Aristotle's Theory of Poetry and Fine Art* (New York: Dover, 1951), p. 355.

chapter many of their insights into characterization will be utilized as material that the classroom teacher may use for topics of discussion or composition. One must be selective in the use of this critical material, however. For, unfortunately, there exists some redundancy within and among the statements of various critics. They often seem to be saying substantially the same things in different ways. At times they are given to taking extreme positions on what seem to be clear and obvious meanings in a work. At other times they seem to be reading more into a work than the work justifies. And at their worst, although one must concede that this may be more the fault of an inaccurate reading of the critic than of the critic himself, they have often confused rather than clarified the central issues under discussion by unduly emphasizing peripheral rather than essential matters of concern. But, this is not necessarily undesirable. Both teachers and students can sharpen their own critical skills through a "critical" reading of the critics. As a court of last resort, however, one can always—or better yet, ought always—consult the text of the work itself.

A final statement on character classification is in order before considering the characters in the central and secondary works of this discussion. In *The Lonely Crowd*[14] David Riesman develops some valuable terms which the teacher may use to assist the student in making finer and subtler distinctions between characters than he can with the terms "round" and "flat." These are the terms: tradition direction, other direction, and inner direction. Riesman's explanation of these terms is complex and at times tedious, and recently has been subjected to disclamations by various sociologists. The accuracy of the terms has been questioned, and in ways which it is not the object of this work to pursue, they have been found deficient. Yet the substance of his classifications has great validity for pedagogical purposes. Riesman provides handy guidelines for comparing and contrasting characters and, even more importantly, for examining the ambivalences within a single character. Many of the characters to be considered here will be made more readily interpretable through an application of these distinctions.

Riesman sees character linked with a "mode of conformity" necessary to preserve and maintain a given culture or society. The tradition-directed character is the greatest conformist of the group. His outlooks

---

[14] David Riesman *et al.*, "Character and Society," in *The Lonely Crowd* (New York: Doubleday & Co., Inc., 1955), pp., 19–48.

remain constant year after year. He has little aptitude or inclination for innovation, and has resigned himself to a static, uneventful life, often attended by much suffering and mistreatment by others in a higher social caste. He is ill-prepared to cope with the dislocations and tensions which any form of progress brings in its wake. He accepts the mores of his society without question, satisfied that they have always been an integral part of his received culture. He accepts the doctrine of stability for its own sake, and is prone to have little or no rebellion potential. According to Riesman, Europe of the Middle Ages or modern India would characterize the phenomenon of tradition direction.

The inner-directed character is in marked contrast to the tradition-directed character. He is a man in a state of transition, usually from tradition direction. He has predominated in the West as a result of the rise of science, economic progress, and the development of free social, political, and religious institutions. His prototype is the Renaissance man,[15] whose personal mobility and desire to achieve self-actualization motivated his entire being. The American pioneer exemplified this type. Nevertheless, the inner-directed person permits tradition to influence his behavior somewhat, although not to determine it. He is also somewhat tradition-directed in the sense that his family group with which he has had immediate and vital contact provides him with a set of values and norms which operate from within him, somewhat intuitively, to attune him to the comprehensiveness and realities of experience, and to guide his future behavior. On the whole, however, he is the real shaper of his destiny, unlike the tradition-directed type.

The other-directed character is best represented by many middle-class Americans. William H. Whyte has labeled him as the "organization man," and Erich Fromm has distinguished him from the autonomous or inner-directed man by labeling him as a "marketer," the mainstay of modern suburbia. He is usually oversocialized, in a constant sweat to outdo the achievements of his neighbors, and engaged in an unending quest to acquire the symbols and realities of social power which will highlight him as a man on the move, or a pseudo-inner-directed type. Unlike the inner-directed man, however, he has no internal intuitional forces to guide his behavior. His family influences do not play so important a role in his life as do those of the inner-directed man. He gets his sense of direction from those about him, whom he sometimes con-

---

[15] One must qualify this statement immediately because Renaissance man was tradition-directed in that he did look with favor to the classical past of Greece and Rome.

descendingly regards as peers and to whom he looks for approval and guidance. Like Arthur Miller's Willy Loman of *Death of a Salesman*, he values being liked as the highest good which one can attain. He is moved by mass media, sensitive to majority opinion and, despite his outward display of vitality and the accomplished rhetoric of his utterances, he often lives a life of quiet desperation, compounded by the complications and frustrations of modern living. At his worst he epitomizes T. S. Eliot's hollow man. To Riesman the other-directed man is in reality a tradition-directed man whose personality has been transformed by the influences of a society that is undergoing rapid change. He would be tradition-directed were he born in a static society.

To summarize, we might say that the tradition-directed man conforms to a mode of behavior determined by received mores, sanctioned and enforced by those in authority about him. To some degree the Trappist monk and the dedicated United States Marine would be further examples to illustrate this type in modern times. One could argue a case for true inner direction, however, for both the monk and the marine, depending on one's point of view. The inner-directed man need not be the direct opposite of the tradition-directed type. For, as Riesman points out, he is neither so completely independent nor autonomous as he seems. He develops some sense of guilt for not always being able to live up to the norms of behavior which his strong family ties have instilled in him, but in the main he manages to resolve this guilt and to come to terms with the realities of life and to maintain his stability of person. Thoreau and Emerson's conception of an ideal man would in many ways exemplify this type. Riesman suggests two appropriate metaphors to distinguish the other-directed man from the inner-directed man—the radar and the gyroscope, respectively. The other-directed man, like a Madison Avenue sampler, sends out signals with his radar, and then adjusts or conforms his behavior according to the feedback he receives. The inner-directed man, on the other hand, has within him a self-regulating gyroscope. His feedback is internalized; it is both generated and interpreted from within, and his behavior is ultimately influenced by these internal signals.

With the foregoing as background, it is possible to organize a nomenclature which can facilitate the classification and interpretation of the young heroes of American fiction as types of character. Before proceeding, however, the following distinctions will be made. The term "hero" carries the popular connotation of the good man who overcomes evil by righting wrongs and redressing grievances. Here the term will be used as a convenient cover term for the central character who may be a protagonist, an antagonist, a passivist, or any combination of these. His intrinsic worth as a person will in no way be qualified or modified by the term. Moreover, few characters submit readily to categorical classification. There is no such thing as a perfectly tradition-, inner-, or other-directed character. The same holds true for the terms round and flat. These are convenient terms used relatively for purposes of analysis. After analysis, however, when we engage in the process of synthesis, the second component of criticism, we often find the terms overlap considerably, and can become ambiguous. Furthermore, some of Riesman's sociological criteria do not apply to many of the characters considered here. But, as the student's critical skills increase, so, too, will his capacity to interpret and appreciate ambiguities, and to discern the disclaimers which always apply to convenient cover terms. The terms are simply means to achieve higher ends; they are not ends in themselves. Our ultimate end, of course, is to turn out a student who can approach a work of literature properly equipped to appreciate the complexities and ambiguities which give it its superiority as a work of art, to have guidelines with which he can compare it to inferior art forms, and for him to do this intelligently and tastefully, and as independently of his teacher as his abilities will permit.

Perhaps the most succinct summary of the character of Huck Finn appears in a statement of Mark Twain's in which he describes the meaning of his novel: "A book of mine in which a sound mind and a deformed conscience come into conflict and conscience loses."[16] This statement could be used for a topic of discussion or composition because it neatly mirrors what actually happens to Huck, and what he finally becomes during the course of the narrative. It is the job of the teacher and the student to trace how this happens.

At the beginning and ending of *The Adventures of Huckleberry Finn*, during those times when Huck is under the influence of Tom Sawyer, Huck is for the most part an other-directed, tradition-directed character. He moves along with events as he does in the attack by the "Arabs" on the Sunday school outing, which Tom Sawyer engineers. Huck himself does not take the initiative in this or in other episodes except to engage in a few arguments with Tom, which the latter always wins.

[16] Mark Twain, in Hook, p. 183.

Paralleling Huck's flatness as a character is Nigger Jim, who is nothing more than a comic butt for the farcical pranks of the boys, who place a five-cent piece within his grasp and lead him to believe that he has been singled out by certain "malign" spiritual forces for special powers and favors which give him status, and make him the envy of all Negroes within knowing distance. Were Mark Twain to continue and complete the book in this tone, it could scarcely have become the great work it was destined to become. At the end of the book in the Phelps' farm incident, we meet again the same Huck Finn under the influence and control of Tom Sawyer, but this time under more farcical and incredible conditions in their attempt to free Nigger Jim (who, ironically, is already free) from a shack in which he is chained like an animal, and to return him to his rightful owner, Miss Watson.

In those central chapters in which Huck and Jim are travelling on the Mississippi and the influence of Tom Sawyer is absent, however, both Huck and Jim undergo a convincing development of character whose details can be traced out in clearly discernible steps. At least three crucial incidents illustrate this progression. One occurs when Jim, after having been deceived into believing that he had only dreamed that Huck was lost in the canoe in a dense fog, suddenly becomes aware that Huck has been telling a tall tale, and as a result is deeply hurt because Huck has taken so lightly Jim's concern over Huck's safety. This definitely illustrates Jim's capacity to feel profoundly and sensitively as a human being, and Huck's capacity to humble himself to a "nigger," an unthinkable act by the standards of their society, and to ask Jim's forgiveness. The innate nobility of each person is dramatically portrayed through this incident.

Another incident occurs when Jim reminisces about his wife and children, from whom he has been brutally separated as a result of his being sold into slavery. He recalls when he scolded and cuffed his young daughter Elizabeth for not closing a door when he ordered her to, only to discover moments later that she was deaf. He is overcome with grief and shame over his action, and the poignancy of his feelings reveals the true dignity of his nature, and thoroughly discredits the popularly held notion on which Huck had been nurtured, that the Negro Slave is mere chattel property, a sub-human entity. The teacher ought at this time to read to his students a short statement by Ralph Ellison,[17] a modern

---

[17] Ralph Ellison," The Negro Writer in America: An Exchange," *Partisan Review*, XXV (Spring, 1958), pp. 212–22.

Negro writer, who severely criticizes the beginning and ending of *The Adventures of Huckleberry Finn* because of their portrayal of Jim as a stereotyped Negro minstrel, a thoroughly flat character who, in effect, is too dehumanized to be either tradition-, other-, or inner-directed. One has a tendency to feel, however, that Ellison is overstating his case. He fails to realize that Mark Twain makes the white man appear even more ridiculous, despite the indignities that Jim suffers. Even at his "flattest" Jim does maintain his basic humility and dignity, however tarnished they may be by farce. And in the final scenes of the book Jim does display a remarkable sense of selflessness and loyalty when he risks his own safety to assist Tom, who has been wounded by a gun shot. No white person involved in this series of bizarre episodes, even Huck himself, ever rises to this height of nobility.

The third incident, which is really the climax of the entire narrative, occurs when Huck discovers that he cannot "pray a lie." Though Huck often does lie, as he does when he encounters Mrs. Loftus, the Wilks girls, the bounty hunters, and others, his lies are ordinarily those of a prankster and a tall-tale teller, who is exercising his vivid imagination with no intention of doing any harm, but rather, in some cases, of effecting some positive good, such as saving Jim from being returned to slavery, or preventing the drowning of three hardened criminals on the sinking river boat, the *Walter Scott*. He is incapable of lying to himself, however, or of succumbing to the big lie on which the justification for slavery rests. At this point Huck discards the radar and relies on the gyroscope. He moves decisively from other direction and tradition direction to inner direction.

Huck is an amazing character in that he lives in a world festering with evil, but he does not permit this evil to contaminate him personally. In this respect he is far more capable of resolving the contradictions and confusions of the world about him than many of the other young heroes being considered here. His greatest virtue is his inability to hate; or, to put it in Christian-Socratic terms, he truly lives up to the dictum that it is far better to have evil done to oneself than to commit evil. It is this attitude which helps him to maintain his mental balance and to keep a firm grasp on reality.

Nevertheless, Huck is not without his failings. He displays poor judgment in placing the rattlesnake skin next to Jim, who is asleep. This causes Jim to be bitten by the dead rattlesnake's mate and almost causes his death. When the raft is hit by the river steamer and Huck and Jim are separated, Huck, after reaching shore, seems to be but little concerned over the fate of Jim, to whom he has become deeply attached while on the raft. And whenever Jim exults over the possibility of gaining his freedom, Huck becomes mysteriously resentful and irritable.

Huck stands in sharp contrast to many of the other characters in the novel. Next to the Duke, the Dauphin, and Pap Finn he is the equivalent of a canonized saint. Though these men brutally mistreat him, he yet takes a kindly and tolerant attitude toward them, while he knows objectively that they are "rapscallions" and scoundrels. Though he admires the Shepherdsons and Grangerfords for their natural nobility, generosity, and courage, he rises above them in his ability to compromise issues sanely and sensibly. He knows that at times it is better to bend than to break. He has a sense of pride, but it is tempered by enough humility to prevent his becoming obsessed with fixed ideas as the Shepherdsons and Grangerfords do in their insane feud. He stands in sharp contrast, too, to most of the townsfolk, who take sadistic delight in running helpless women out of town on rails, tying cans to dogs' tails to watch them run themselves to death, or watching a circus clown, who seems not to know what he is doing, ride a horse at great peril to his life. Huck reveals his character most tenderly after the final ravages of the feud. Viewing the many mutilated bodies, he thinks of his young friend, Buck Grangerford, who has been killed in the havoc. Huck weeps (the only time he does in the novel) and it is apparent that this nightmarish experience will affect him for life, but it does not drive him to cynicism. Huck is in the audience when Colonel Sherburn makes his vitriolic speech to the townsfolk, who cower and sneak away. Sherburn's remarks on the cowardice and duplicity of the average man do not apply to Huck, however. One really cannot view Huck as part of the audience. It is more accurate to say that he is a detached observer who overhears the speech. Huck's inability to hate is matched only by his humility and modesty. Through humility he is able to see himself for what he really is—no more, no less. The attainment of humility is the highest form of self-realization and gives one undistorted insights into reality. As for his modesty, a quote from Bergson should prove adequate as a definition: "True modesty can be nothing but a meditation on vanity. It springs from the sights of others' mistakes, and the dread of being similarly deceived. . . . In short it is an acquired virtue."[18]

[18] Bergson, in Wyler, p. 172.

Whenever appropriate, Huck Finn will be used as the standard of reference to which other characters will be compared and contrasted. Holden Caulfield of *The Catcher in the Rye* compares and contrasts significantly with Huck Finn. Like *The Adventures of Huckleberry Finn*, this book has been subjected to much critical interpretation. Holden's situation is far more complicated (though not necessarily more complex) than Huck's. Edgar Branch hits the mark when he says, "Whereas Huck is the sexless pre-adolescent, Holden is the sex-conscious boy who yearns for the uncomplicated state of Huck."[19] He seems to be somewhat off the mark, however, when he states that Huck and Holden are equally charitable and innocent, and "As with Huck, his [Holden's] humility ironically reveals his goodness and integrity."[20] Branch bases these conclusions on the fact that Holden is righteously shocked when he sees obscene four-letter words on public walls, and that he displays a childlike innocence in his love of play-acting and story telling, as does Huck. The fact is that these four-letter words are doubtless part of the working vocabulary of the boys at Pency Prep, along with less objectionable words like "bastard" and "goddam." That Salinger does not put the word in Holden's mouth as a common item of his vocabulary, does not rule out the certainty that he uses it profusely and uninhibitedly. One would have to be quite naive to believe otherwise, or quite unreasonable to demand textual proof as documentation. Blotner and Gwynn go so far as to describe Holden as "actually a saintly, Christian person."[21] The fact is that Holden is actually an intensely other-directed person who is making a desperate effort to become an inner-directed person, but is unable to make the transition. As a result he suffers tensions and frustrations which exhaust him physically and mentally, and render him pitifully unstable. Few characters in fiction display the kinds of ambivalence that Holden does. For this reason he is by no means a flat character. All his impressions and reactions take on a significance worthy of close analysis and interpretation. The typical high school student ordinarily sees Huck Finn as a "good guy," a clever, imaginative, independent person with whom one could easily make friends. The high school student's attitude toward Holden Caulfield is not this

[19] Edgar Branch, "Mark Twain and J. D. Salinger: A "Study in Literary Continuity," *American Quarterly*, IX (Summer, 1957), p. 147.

[20] *Ibid.*, p. 151.

[21] Joseph L. Blotner and Frederick L. Gwynn, *The Fiction of J. D. Salinger* (Pittsburgh: The University of Pittsburgh Press, 1958), p. 29.

simple. He usually finds Holden disturbing and unfathomable in some ways, but in other ways a person with whom one can identify and sympathize. Holden does not yield to easy classification. He leaves many young readers with mixed reactions.

On the one hand, Holden displays many admirable traits which give him the substance to become a truly inner-directed person. He honestly and sincerely wants to be loved, but suffers a sort of paralysis whenever he tries to realize his desire. He has a capacity to love which he can neither project nor express to others, except for his sister Phoebe. Thus in his attempts to love and be loved he ends up either antagonizing people, or being driven to such impulsive behavior as giving ten dollars to two nuns whom he meets in a depot. He sympathizes with the underdog, as he does with James Castle, who jumps from a window and kills himself rather than apologize to a group of bullying boys, one of whom he has mildly insulted. He tells a tall tale to the mother of one of his classmates, Ernest Morrow, whom he really considers to be "as sensitive as a goddam toilet seat," in an effort to convince her that her son is a lovable, modest boy who very humbly has refused a nomination to a prestigious school office. Perhaps his noblest trait is his ability to see through the phoniness and sham of things, and in this respect he has a real prophetic insight into the world about him, although his insights are often overstated and distorted.

These traits notwithstanding, however, Holden is simply unable to adapt to his environment, or to exercise any control over his destiny as Huck Finn has done. Ihab H. Hassan sees Holden as a modern Don Quixote in search of a "simple truth," but continuously thwarted in his efforts by chaos, contradiction, and misunderstanding.[22] Hassan's insight serves to bring Riesman's distinctions of character full circle. For Holden is an other-directed person in search of inner direction but constitutionally better suited for the "simplicity" of a tradition-directed society. This would be in line with Riesman's contention that the other-directed man is in reality a tradition-directed man whom circumstance has placed in a mobile, dynamic society. In a very real sense, Holden, like Dreiser's Clyde Griffiths whom we shall consider later, lives in a society over which he has little control. In so far as that society is corrupt and exploitative Holden becomes a victim of the values of that society, and in this sense *The Catcher in the Rye* is a novel of social protest.

[22] Ihab H. Hassan, "Rare Quixotic Gesture: The Fiction of J. D. Salinger," *The Western Review*, XXI (Summer, 1957), pp. 261–80.

The student is aware, too, however, that Holden has a seamier side to his character. He is, as Robert O. Bowen portrays him, an aberrant and a grotesque person in some ways.[23] He morbidly emphasizes distasteful traits in others—Ackley's halitosis, Stradlater's untidy razor, Mr. Spencer's ratty bathrobe and aged flesh. There is an incident in which he intentionally enrages Ackley by playing blind and calling him, "Mother, darling." But he will brook no teasing from others. He is insanely jealous of Stradlater's virility, and becomes enraged when he thinks that Stradlater may have "given the time" to Jane Gallagher, a girl who would not let Holden kiss her on the mouth. He condemns the movies as "phony" and yet waits in long lines to see them. His attachment to his brother Allie, who has been dead for three years, is curiously unnatural, and his sustained guilt for not letting Allie join him on a bike ride before his death borders on irrationality. Though a professed puritan who cannot "give the time" to just any girl, he readily arranges for the services of a call girl with whom he is unable to consummate the sex act. Holden is more than just simply "a sixteen year old lad whose vivid encounter with everyday life is tragically humorous—or humorously tragic."[24] He is in a state of deep despair, and is well on his way to the great, "bottomless fall" which Mr. Antolini later tells him about.

There are many clues which foreshadow his deterioration. Two crucial incidents will illustrate. The first occurs when he is with Sally Hayes, the "butt twitching" teaser with whom he has managed to get a date after his arrival in New York. Overpowered by an utterly irrational impulse, he asks her to run off with him to live in Vermont where they can chop wood and live an idyllic life. But it is really an act of sheer desperation. The frustrations of existence itself have become too much for Holden to endure, and the evening ends disastrously when Sally leaves him for his overbearing manner, and for shouting vulgarities at her. In this incident Holden's behavior is totally inconsistent with the behavior ordinarily expected of a rational person.

The second incident, which is even more crucial, occurs when Holden visits Mr. Antolini, a former teacher of his whom he respects because he was not concerned about getting blood on his clothes when

[23] Robert O. Bowen," The Salinger Syndrome: Charity Against Whom? "*Ramparts*, 1 (May, 1962), pp. 52–60.
[24] Arthur Heiserman and James E. Miller, Jr., "J. D. Salinger: Some Crazy Cliff," *Western Humanities Review*, X (Spring, 1956), p. 134.

he attended to James Castle, who died from the injuries of his jump. This incident is the major climax of the work. In it Salinger's rhetoric is at its best, and Holden's character reveals itself in its fullness. The incident is fraught with ambiguities and uncertainties, but there is one certainty which becomes blindingly clear: Holden has reached the nadir of his psychic deterioriation.

The incident provides, too, an expanded insight into the puzzling character of Mr. Antolini who, together with Phoebe, is next to Holden the most fully developed character in the book. An English teacher, Antolini is given to excessive verbalization. His facility with words is extremely annoying to Holden. He speaks wittily and knowledgeably of books and ideas and, like Mr. Spencer earlier, he subjects Holden to an extended "lecture," but at a more sophisticated level. He senses Holden's distress, and tries to comfort him by pointing out that men throughout history have undergone the same experience and have profited from it. Some of these men have been gifted enough to record their experiences for all of us to share. He then climaxes his "lecture" with the aphoristic quote, "The mark of the immature man is that he wants to die nobly for a cause, while the mark of a mature man is that he wants to live humbly for one."[25] In Holden's state words bring him little comfort. Philosophy cannot cure a toothache. There is little that Antolini says that really applies to Holden's case, anyhow. So, in a sense, he makes a verbal fool of himself. Antolini then prepares a bed on the couch for Holden to stay overnight, and later Holden awakens to find Antolini stroking his head. Holden's reaction is to interpret this act as a homosexual advance, and much to Mr. Antolini's discomfort he leaves the apartment hastily.

This incident is crucial for two reasons. First, there is no definite evidence that Antolini is making a homosexual advance, though one cannot be absolutely certain of this. Antolini's action could just as easily have been a simple, spontaneous, caressing touch, by no means unusual under the circumstances. A man who does not mind getting blood on his clothes to attend to a dead boy, could reasonably be expected to tousle a boy's head, or to put an affectionate hand on him with no intention of soliciting a homosexual response. Probably Wings Biddlebaum in Anderson's *Winesburg, Ohio*, is no homosexual, and the caresses he gives to his students, which ultimately lead to his brutal mistreat-

[25] J. D. Salinger, *The Catcher in the Rye* (New York: Bantam, 1964), p. 188.

ment by the townsfolk, are far more intimate than Antolini's. Furthermore, when Holden reconsiders the matter later, he admits that he might have grossly misinterpreted Antolini's act. But Holden has deteriorated psychologically to such an extent that he is not completely responsible for his judgments. He is, in fact, practically in a state of shock. For these reasons it seems unreasonable that on the evidence available some critics state categorically that Antolini is homosexual. Bowen states, "Mr. Antolini does have a social flaw, though: he is homosexual."[26] Edgar Branch in the article cited earlier states substantially the same.

Secondly, let us grant for the sake of the argument that Mr. Antolini is homosexual. Then does this not indicate a serious failing in Holden's character, in that he lacks the charity and understanding to sympathize with a man who, despite his minor faults and his major flaw of character, has demonstrated himself worthy of respect in every other way? Holden consistently insists on perfection in others, but is often myopic in regard to his own failings. The encounter with Antolini dramatically illustrates his intolerance of frailty in others, and his unreasonableness in expecting others to provide him with comfort and security in his hour of need. This is scarcely the stuff of which saints are made. How different from Huck Finn is Holden in this respect. Huck never says a disparaging word of Pap, though he fears him. Certainly Jim realizes that Huck would have been upset had he known that Pap Finn was the dead man on the house raft. Huck feels sorry for the Duke and the Dauphin, who are run out of town on a rail—even after these men have exploited him to a degree infinitely greater than Holden had ever been exploited, even by the finger-flicking bellhop Maurice, much less Antolini. There is irony in Edgar Branch's observation that "Huck can always depend on Jim; their physical relationship is consciously innocent. But Mr. Antolini is Holden's last refuge in his disintegrating world."[27] Branch clearly misses the converse point that Mr. Antolini could never depend on Holden as Jim can depend on Huck. And in this way, Huck and Holden are sharply contrasted characters.

All of this is not to say, however, that Huck and Holden are antithetical characters. As Huck's greatest virtue is his inability to hate, and from this stem his other virtues, Holden's greatest failing is his in-

[26] Bowen, p. 58.
[27] Branch, p. 144.

ability to resolve through charity the frustrations and contradictions which bedevil him. For Holden does not really hate those of whom he speaks so bitterly, nor those who so easily disillusion him. He craves to love and be loved, but he is unable to translate this desire into action, and this inability eventually proves his undoing. Huck is never undone by the persons or circumstances that he becomes involved with. There is something in his nature which gives him this adaptability—something which suggests some ultimately unanswerable questions about the nature of the human character. Neither a close study of the texts under consideration nor the insights of professional critics provide completely satisfactory answers to these questions. The naturalists (of whom, more later) suggest some answers through the workings of heredity, environment, and chance.

Stephen Crane's Henry Fleming, in *The Red Badge of Courage*, gives us a glimpse of a type of character who in one sense is completely different from either Huck or Holden. At the beginning of his career as a developing character he is other-directed in a way that Huck and Holden are not. He lacks inner direction in that his family influences do little to direct his motivation. He is needed on the farm to help his widowed mother, but chooses instead to enlist in the Union Army and gain the glory he has read about in the newspapers, and recalls from his studies of the Greek epics in grammar school. He is sensitive to the fact that other young men are enlisting, and that the young girls in his community admire the fighting man. Like Huck and Holden, he ventures into the unknown, but he does so at a much greater risk to his personal safety. Unlike Huck and Holden, he does not act impulsively. He thinks out carefully what he intends to do, and then takes decisive action and enlists. Once in the army, during periods of enforced idleness, he becomes reflective and philosophical. Huck reflects very little; he takes situations as they present themselves, and then, thinking on his feet, resolves the problems accordingly. Occasionally, he is given to thinking things out, as when he evaluates his Sunday school teachings, or when he considers Pap's distinctions between "stealing" and "borrowing"; but on the whole he is more inclined toward action than thought. Holden indulges in thoughts that encompass abstract questions, not directly related to the empirical world about him. For example, he will pose the imponderable question of where the ducks go in the winter. Unlike Henry Fleming, he does not come to grips with the question of who he is, and what he must prove to himself to establish his identity, though this is what he should be doing. Though he is self-centered, he is not intro-spective in the way Henry Fleming is. His radar predominates over his gyroscope. Fleming's gyroscope is always in operation trying to blank out his radar. Holden cannot even rationalize his behavior. He is com-pletely incapable of answering Phoebe's simple question when she asks him to name one thing he "really" likes.

Though other-directed, Henry Fleming has a purpose and a goal which eventually lead him to inner direction. During the times that the army is idle he wonders what his worth will be when he confronts the enemy. His radar is in full operation when he questions the other soldiers about him and notes their responses. He always ends up with the im-pression that he is inferior to those about him. When his test does come and he takes flight like the "proverbial chicken," his ego is badly shat-tered. As a result he suffers the intense guilt of the inner-directed man, and the other-directed element of his character causes him to become greatly concerned about what others will think of him. Henry cannot accept this image of himself in its full implications. Thus, he indulges in a series of rationalizations unparalleled by any thought processes that Huck or Holden indulge in. He justifies his flight as an act of "higher wisdom," which his comrades are utterly incapable of, and he receives corroboration from nature when a squirrel takes flight after he throws a pine cone at it. After all, he argues inwardly, the law of self-preserva-tion has a high priority in human actions; but he conveniently dis-misses the fact that fidelity to one's commitments has a higher priority. In terms easily accessible to the high school student, Henry is doing a good job of kidding himself. Crane develops Henry's internal dialectic in finely graded steps of progression, whose main points can easily be outlined and discerned.

As he makes his way back to his regiment he receives by accident a head bruise as a result of being hit with the rifle butt of a panicky soldier from whom he tries to get information. When he returns to his regiment, his comrades interpret his head wound as a battle wound, and Henry, much to his surprise, is received as a hero. His shattered ego now in good repair, he tends to scorn the men around him, but like Huck Finn who cannot pray a lie, Henry cannot live a lie. He becomes thoroughly disgusted with his earlier cowardice and goes on to prove himself decisively in the next battle. At the end of the novel, Crane in language that literally gushes, describes Henry's initiation into inner direction. But he becomes an inner-directed man more by accident and instinct than by rational design.

Henry Fleming is the prototype of the untried man who is eager to incur the risks involved in establishing his identity. His development parallels the development of the loud soldier, Wilson, but at a more complex level. Each of the men undergoes a metamorphosis of character. The student ought to discern clearly that the two men are more different at the end of the novel than they were at the beginning, and to be able to trace the means by which these differences are brought about. Crane presents his material directly and clearly enough for this to be no really difficult task for the student who is willing to make the application. It should be noted, too, that Crane does not clutter or confuse his account by including matters which are not essential to the development of character. Thus, the motive of patriotism does not affect Henry in any way, and statements on the backgrounds, causes, or justifications for the Civil War are conspicuously absent from the text. The character under stress and his reactions to his circumstances are the main concern of the work.

As a person, Billy Budd is radically different from any of the other characters thus far considered. If he is examined out of context and isolated from the other elements of *Billy Budd*, he becomes something of a flat, tradition-directed character. Like Claggart, he is really more an idea than a person, though one would not want to stretch this concept too far because each of the men does have individual features. Except in a mystical sense which is suggested by his mysterious conversation with Vere the night before his hanging, and his blessing to Vere just before he hangs, he shows no signs of growth in his career as a character. Melville *presents* him more than he *develops* him. There are many puzzling and contradictory elements in his nature. Though having lived all his nineteen years in the corrupted environment of the waterfront, he shows no evidence of personal corruption. He is utterly naive and unsophisticated. He is depicted as an angelic being who except for his stutter is unflawed by the curse of Adam. He is innocent of the ways of men, and unable to associate with them in any complex relationship. His good humor, easygoing nature, and pristine simplicity give him an air of perfection which suggests the qualities of Rousseau's ideal type, the noble savage who is untouched by the taints of civilization. His physical proportions are perfect; he is, but for one notable exception, universally loved by all the men aboard ship. His only human failings are his stutter and his readiness to use his fists when badgered, and these failings eventually prove his undoing.

In contrast to Billy Budd is John Claggart. As Billy is divine, Claggart is Satanic. Though a man of superior intellect and good physical proportions, there is a mystique about him which, Melville tells us, is a manifestation of his "innate depravity." It soon becomes obvious that he hates Billy for no apparent reason but to hate for its own sake, and Billy becomes the perfect object of this hatred, which smolders within him. Melville tells us directly of his nature, but we do not see him in the fullness of his evil until he utters the fantastic accusation that Billy has been fomenting a mutiny—an outright and shameless lie.

Melville goes to great pains to highlight Billy's goodness and Claggart's evil—so much so that were it not for Vere, the story would approach pure allegory. In effect, Billy and Claggart are functionaries who serve to bring out the one rounded character of the story, Captain Vere. Vere is a real person who must make a particular decision to bring about justice in an imperfect world where absolute justice becomes impossible. Billy and Claggart respectively represent absolute goodness and absolute evil. They are more archetypal than individual. One could almost say they are hypothetical. They represent opposing forces which can be assigned only to universal man, not individual men, who in the common run of experience represent various admixtures of good and evil. Yet Melville presents Billy and Claggart so powerfully and the situation that they create is so intensely dramatic that from an impressionistic or subjective point of view they sometimes appear real; but from an objective point of view they are not. Vere, however, is real, and his predicament is real. He is faced with the problem of determining and choosing the lesser of two evils. By permitting Billy to be hanged he is violating justice by condemning an innocent man. But were he to dismiss the case or to defer it until a higher authority could judge it, he would be endangering the common good by making it possible for mutiny and civil strife to run rampant. The teacher can make this clear to the student by examining other literature in which men are faced with similar dilemmas. The Isaac-Abraham or Pilate-Christ situations would serve as excellent examples. In current times Harry Truman's decision to employ the atomic bomb would serve as an even better example.

It is ironic that the character who gives the title to Melville's work is not a real character in an aesthetic sense, but he serves to provide the occasion for a real character to demonstrate himself. The student must see that only in art can this be done. Billy and Claggart are as impersonal as the atomic bomb; but Vere is as real as President Truman. The foregoing analogy, like all analogies, has its logical weaknesses. Analogies are excellent pedagogical devices, however, if the student can be convinced that they serve to clarify, not to prove, an assumption that logic often cannot clarify.

It is fascinating to note how critics have evaluated Captain Vere as a person by virtue of his decisions. Two examples will suffice for the moment. Leonard Caspar views him as an unnaturally monstrous man, "a victim of mental aberration."[28] But Milton Stern views him as a true tragic character, who is forced by circumstances beyond his control to serve a higher good against his conscience and in violation of his personal feelings.[29] The Vere problem will be treated more fully in subsequent chapters.

The remainder of this chapter will concern itself with salient points from some of the secondary works in which characterization is of significance as a topic of study. Whenever appropriate, references will be made to characters of the central works with whom there is some relationship which can be employed for pedagogical purposes, and needed plot summary will be provided.

In Lionel Trilling's "Of This Time, of That Place," there are three characters whose relationships bear some similarities to those of Vere, Billy, and Claggart. Joseph Howe is a first-year English teacher in a small liberal arts college, and Tertan and Blackburn are his students. Tertan is much like Billy in that he is naive, selfless, and sincere; Blackburn is treacherous and dishonest, perhaps as perfect an example of the worst kind of other-directed character one could find in fiction. He is involved in campus activities, a grade grubber, and in every way thoroughly obnoxious. He can be compared easily to Stradlater in *The Catcher in the Rye*. Tertan, on the other hand, is a serious student who inspires something of a father complex in Howe, but the lad is obviously psychologically disordered; he writes incoherently and in "tor-

---

[28] Leonard Caspar, "The Case Against Captain Vere," *Perspective*, V (Summer, 1952), p. 150.

[29] Milton R. Stern, *The Fine-Hammered Steel of Herman Melville* (Urbana: The University of Illinois Press, 1957), pp. 26–27.

rential prose" (Trilling provides generous samplings which students can examine). He is always on the verge of making sense, but never quite does so. At the end of the school year, Howe has to watch Tertan drop out of school, while Blackburn, who has been able to bluff his way through courses, graduates and is made an offer by a business firm for a position which has a promising future. Tertan is obviously headed for the sanitarium. The student can compare Vere's and Howe's situations, and the webs of circumstance which render them helpless, despite their positions of authority and responsibility.

Clyde Griffiths of Dreiser's *An American Tragedy* is another example of an other-directed person in an agonized search for his identity. There is little in him that can be admired; at best he must be pitied. He lies, fakes, and pretends in an effort to acquire comfort, security, and social status. He even plans to murder a helpless girl, Roberta Alden, whom he has made pregnant, and although the circumstances which lead up to the culmination of the act are clouded with uncertainty as to his actual guilt, he is guilty by virtue of his intentions and deliberations. When under the influence of the young minister while he is in death row, Clyde does give evidence of some qualities of character that could lead to his rehabilitation, but societal mores are stacked too heavily against him, and he is finally executed.

Clyde Griffiths stands in sharp contrast to Huck Finn, who goes so far as to repudiate a $6000 legacy and the pressures of a false society to live a life of penurious ease on the River. Clyde is not even aware of the falseness of his society; even if he were, however, he would still want to become a part of it. There is never any question of his responsibility for his predicament. He is a conscious plotter who is ever aware of what he is doing and the consequences that attend his actions. Yet he is not without conscience, although he does everything in his power to still its workings in him. He is more a victim of himself than he is of circumstances or society. Dreiser himself makes us aware of Clyde's failings in a summary statement:

For to say the truth, Clyde had a soul that was not destined to grow up. He lacked decidedly that mental clarity and inner-directing application that in so many permits them to sort out from the facts and avenues of life the particular thing or things that make for direct advancement.[30]

[30] Theodore Dreiser, *An American Tragedy* (Cleveland: World Publishing, 1962), p. 189.

And, Clyde is unable to compensate for his failings in any socially acceptable way. Unlike Huck Finn, Clyde does not have the humility to accept himself for what he really is, and thus accept his proper station in life.

Yet one cannot be too hard on him. Nature is mysterious in apportioning talents and capacities among human beings. Not all men are emotionally equal or equally capable of coping with the frustrations of life. Certainly one must say in Clyde's favor that, unlike Claggart, he does not do evil for its own sake; but rather to attain an end not intrinsically wrong in itself. Nor is he in the same position as Captain Vere, who seems to have no other choice in his decision. When Clyde's defense attorney attempts to plead a case of moral cowardice on his behalf, he is advancing a partially valid argument. It is invalid, too, however, in that the reader knows that Clyde had carefully planned the murder, and had fully intended to carry it out. The jury is not so certain of this as the reader, but even the reader is left with some shadow of doubt. For Dreiser creates an uncomfortably improbable accident at the climactic moment which obscures and complicates the basic issue of Clyde's degree of guilt. This is a bothersome incident to which the student would do well to give a great deal of thought. One could compare it with the incident in *The Adventures of Huckleberry Finn* when Col. Sherburn kills Old Man Boggs. Sherburn's degree of guilt is hard to determine. He gave fair warning, and he has to live up to his word in order to save face. But, on the other hand, Boggs is drunk and helpless, and Sherburn acts deliberately and intentionally. A final complication enters when one considers that guilt is meaningless unless the guilty party can be brought to justice. Clyde certainly is brought to justice, but no one can enforce justice in Sherburn's case; therefore, he is entitled to freedom. Students will often engage in spirited arguments, pro and con, on this incident; but few can agree with each other as to what course of action would best serve justice. Nevertheless, these are decisions we must all try to come to.

James T. Farrell's Studs Lonigan shares many traits with Clyde Griffiths: he is immoral, inordinately motivated to become successful in the world, and shows little potential for true humility or personal growth. But he is far more brutalized than Clyde, despite the latter's dastardly mistreatment of Roberta Alden. Studs is utterly unrefined and dissolute; he violently hates Negroes and Jews and is carried away by the anti-Germanic hysteria of World War I; his Catholic education does little to improve his character or to give him a sense of piety. Clyde Griffiths is a sensitive, well-mannered young man; Studs is sickeningly squeamish. He is boorish at social functions; disgustingly inarticulate when trying to communicate with others; except for a slight flicker of conscience, he has no scruples about kicking a Jewish boy, Schwartz, in the groin during a football game and almost killing him; he engages in a brutal fist fight with his younger brother. At twenty-three he is obese and beginning to lose his health. Before he is thirty, he gets in a fist fight with Weary, whom he had beaten when they were boys, and ends up prostrate and wallowing in his vomit. In a foolish effort to strike a bonanza he squanders money on the stock market and suffers a financial disaster. Yet in his early thirties he has a unique opportunity to reverse the failings of his lifetime when Catherine Bannion, whom he has known since childhood, and he fall in love and make arrangements to marry. This relationship seems to mellow Studs, but in time he finds her repulsive because she does not have enough "class" for him, and in the worst act that he commits he literally tears off her clothing and violates her one evening while they are sitting together on a couch. Catherine becomes pregnant, but before they can marry, Studs' health deteriorates so completely that he dies. Then Catherine becomes an object of abuse at the hands of Studs' family, who accuses her of "seducing" him and thus contributing to his death.

The criteria of the naturalists do not apply to Studs completely. Like Clyde, he is more a victim of himself than of the forces about him. He has advantages in life that Huck Finn could never enjoy: a good father, a chance to acquire a good education, and an opportunity to take advantage of the economic boom of the 1920's, as his Jewish brother-in-law does. Studs proves completely unequal to these opportunities, however. There seems to be an intrinsic rottenness in Studs which defies conventional interpretations. During the 1930's tʰ Southern Agrarians (who have modified their position considera since 1945) would have attributed Studs' difficulties to the corrup ng influence of urbanism. But the solution is not so simple. There is ore to Studs' depravity than the effects attributable to his environment. Although the book is readable and comprehensible to the young student, he is likely to become thoroughly depressed with a character like Studs Lonigan, who has little in him to admire. Any sympathy one might have for Studs would have to stem more from one's sense of humanitarianism and charity than from anything Studs does to earn it.

After reading *Studs Lonigan*, the student can profit greatly from a reading of *Martin Eden* because of the many similarities and contrasts which can be drawn between the heroes whose names title these books. Up to the point in his life when he comes into contact with the Morse family, who invite him for a visit after he saves one of their sons from a beating, Martin shares many features in common with Studs. An ordinary seaman, whose only world is the rough-and-tumble waterfronts of San Francisco at the turn of the century, Martin is typically uncouth, uneducated, and given to brawling. His association with the Morse family proves a pivotal point in his career. This occurs through Ruth Morse, who is a student at Stanford and, in Martin's eyes, the epitome of the cultured woman. Falling helplessly in love with her, he goes on a crash program to become her equal in education and refinement. He reads voraciously, and becomes conscious of his personal habits (he brushes his teeth for the first time). In doing all this, he exerts a force of will and a sense of idealism of which Studs would be totally incapable. In time Martin becomes highly educated, a skillful writer who, after suffering many reverses, eventually hits the big market with his essays and stories, and achieves outstanding financial success and fame. Paralleling this remarkable accomplishment, however, is his growing realization that Ruth Morse is really a flat person and a debilitated bourgeois (London uses the work as a sounding board to advance his doctrines of socialism). Her college education is an academic fraud, and her cultural station in life a hollow mockery. Thus, despite his success, he suffers a terrible disillusionment. He finds himself in limbo. He is too refined and wealthy to return to his life on the waterfronts, but too disgusted with the sham and dishonesty of the Morses to feel at home in their world, though his success eventually makes him a very desirable person in their eyes. He has but one alternative—suicide. Both Farrell and London depict the death scenes of Studs and Martin in graphic, dramatic detail. The student could profit from studying these scenes carefully. They suggest that had Studs had Martin's strength of will and sense of high idealism, he might have lived a happy, productive life. On the other hand, had Martin never left the waterfront, his life might not have become so complicated.

Saul Bellow's Augie March can best be summed up as a Studs Lonigan with intelligence, sensitivity, and imagination He lacks Studs' obtuseness and boorishness In classifying him as a character type, one would have to conclude that he is completely non-tradition-directed (except for his attachment to great books of the past), and that he has effected as neat a synthesis of inner and other direction in his own person as one could achieve He is his own man; his gyroscope is continuously in operation. He also has a radar system, however, which tunes him in on the wavelengths of those about him. Often this leads to rewarding situations for him, as in his relationships with Einhorn, the successful entrepreneur who sets him up as his private secretary, and provides him with extensive material comforts At other times his radar system gets him into difficulties because of a conflict between it and the gyroscope This occurs when he pursues the mad adventure with his psychoneurotic friend Thea to travel to Mexico with a wild eagle which they intend to train as a lizard-killer. The relationship deteriorates when the eagle "chickens out" and Augie and Thea are unfaithful to each other. Augie's marriage later proves a nightmarish experience for him, also.

Augie is a much more complex character than either Studs Lonigan or Martin Eden. He seduces the reader into liking him, even though he is at heart a thoroughly immoral person. He steals, lies, cheats, and is incapable of sustained guilt. Bellow plays down this side of his nature, but it is the teacher's responsibility to make the student aware of the real Augie March.

The characters of some of our young heroes are often revealed in their relationships with their fathers. Huck Finn has already been mentioned in this regard. There are others who merit consideration. Young Jody of Steinbeck's *The Red Pony* has to endure an authoritarian, sometimes tyrannical father who causes him anxiety and tension, and doubtless contributes to the boy's hypersensitivity. In Faulkner's "Barn Burning" young Sarty Snopes has a relationship with his father reminiscent of the chamber-of-horrors experience which Huck endures under Pap Finn. In Faulkner's account, however, the horror is unrelieved by humor as it is in Twain's. Sarty's character reveals itself most tellingly when he has to choose between his conscience and filial obedience as his father sets out with malice in his heart to burn a barn for being "wronged." His conscience overcomes his loyalty to his father, and he thus becomes the direct cause of his father's being shot. The pathos of his grief serves to classify him as a thoroughly round character who easily earns our sympathy and admiration. Ab Snopes, the father, is so completely dehumanized as to defy classification, but it is a tribute to Faulkner's art, as it is to Melville's, that Ab Snopes, like Billy Budd and Claggart, is experienced by the reader as a very real person. In

Hemingway's "Fathers and Sons" we encounter a peculiar father-son relationship. Nick Adams' father is a medical doctor who has some strange notions about sex which tend to puzzle Nick and encourage him to engage in some heterosexual experimentation on his own. He speaks to Nick of masturbation causing blindness, of human beings having sexual relations with animals, and of the great Enrico Caruso who perversely stimulated women with a potato masher. Nick is soundly whipped when he refuses to wear his father's underwear. Yet despite his father's eccentricities, Nick maintains a real loyalty to him. Years later when he speaks to his own son of his father, he praises him as a great hunter, and never says anything disparaging of him. One gets the impression that Nick has more understanding towards his son than his father had for him, as evidenced by the free give-and-take of their conversation.

Many adolescent boys have strained relations with their fathers that teachers and guidance counselors are not aware of. Discussions of this problem through the medium of literature ought to be most helpful in aiding these students to understand their own problems. At least, this ought to be one of the end results of a study of literature, although it cannot be the entire justification for its study.

Willa Cather's short story "Paul's Case" is high-priority reading for the serious teenager. Few adults, teachers included, are aware that the problems Paul faces and his reactions to the world about him are typical in varying degrees of the problems modern youth faces—though often their outward actions belie this reality. Paul is a master at the art of contempt. The contempt of many young people for adults is less obvious, but no less real. Paul displays his contempt through such well-developed mannerisms as twitching his lips, sneering, raising his eyebrows, and smiling unctuously and incessantly. At school, whenever he is called to the office for misbehavior, he takes great pains short of violence to make his teachers hate him, and is delighted whenever he succeeds. There is another side to Paul, however, which is not so obvious. He lives with his father in a dingy bare apartment which he finds odious, and he has a job as an usher at the concert hall which he performs as an impresario to the satisfaction of all the patrons. Home and school are hell to him, but the concert hall is his sanctuary—the one oasis in the desert that symbolizes his life. As one would expect, Paul is expelled from school, and goes to work as a messenger for a business concern. Then one day he decides to live an intense and final weekend. He absconds with a bundle of cash one Friday, and goes to New York where he lives in luxury in a plush suite—eating the finest food and drinking the finest drinks. On Monday he reads of his act in the newspapers, and although he learns that his father is willing to make good the loss, and the company is willing not to prosecute, he commits suicide by jumping from an incline into the path of an oncoming train.

High school anthologies ordinarily do not contain enough literature of this kind to which students can respond with interest and sensitivity. Every student is a "Paul" to a degree, and the teacher who would involve his students in stories of this kind is performing a valuable service. Few students could be bored by this kind of a story, as few students can fail to identify with Huck or Holden if they learn of these characters from teachers who are capable of responding to these characters humanely, sympathetically, and when necessary negatively, as they would respond to their own students. Paul, incidentally, exemplifies what Antolini means by the "bottomless fall."

Another example of a youth heading for a "bottomless fall" occurs in Conrad Aiken's "Silent Snow, Secret Snow." Here an adolescent becomes a schizophrenic by degrees. His senses deteriorate; he withdraws from his parents. When he is finally examined by a doctor and questioned about what is bothering him he bursts into a mad giggle. His deterioration is complete when he tells his mother that he hates her and that she is to leave him alone. This story is not so comprehensible to the student as "Paul's Case" or *The Catcher in the Rye* because it is not told with complete straightforwardness; that is, Aiken employs impressionistic imagery to advance the action. With help from the teacher, however, the average student can see the story for what it really is—a horror story like "Paul's Case" in which a youth reaches a point in his life where reality is no longer endurable.

There are yet other kinds of deterioration that characters can experience. One thinks of Truman Capote's *Other Voices, Other Rooms*, in which a thirteen-year-old lad, Joel Knox, is placed in an environment that gradually contributes to his corruption. Joel has his first experience with girls through a tomboy, Idabelle Thompkins, who has lesbian traits, and who embarrasses and humiliates him for his effeminacy. He spends much time with his stepcousin Randolph, an obvious homosexual and transvestite to whom Joel becomes attached emotionally. By the end of the novel it becomes unmistakably clear that Joel is well on his way to becoming a confirmed homosexual. Aside from its unsavory content, the book has some flaws in structure and narrative technique (to be considered in the section on style). Despite these failings, however, it portrays faithfully in discernible degrees the ways in which a young person can be corrupted. Ordinarily, this kind of book is not high school fare. Only in a most progressive and liberal school can a book such as this be studied without serious community repercussions. Nevertheless, the teacher should be familiar with books of this kind, and under some conditions he can suggest it for individual reading.

Yet another type of degenerated character appears in such a work as Jack Kerouac's *On the Road*. Its hero, Sal Paradise, represents the modern beatnik and his vision of life and reality. Sal is an intensely inner-directed type, but his inner direction is a blind, egoistic force. He has a free-wheeling gyroscope which is tuned in for unique, original experiences, and refuses to be affected by conventional morality or the workings of conscience. Other characters in the work are similar to Sal. They are too busy to experience despair or shame. Sal's buddy, Dean Moriarity, sums up this attitude in his statement, "the only people for me are the mad ones, the ones who are mad to live, mad to talk, mad to be saved, desirous of everything at the same time, the ones who never yawn or say a commonplace thing."[31] One would exercise the same caution in presenting this book to high school students as with *Other Voices, Other Rooms*. The book is a basic document on the problems of disoriented youth.

William Faulkner's *Intruder in the Dust* features a character who is in many ways the equivalent of Huck Finn. When Chick Mallison was twelve years old he fell into a creek and was befriended by Lucas Beauchamp, an old Negro who took him into his home where he was fed and his clothes were dried. Chick spends four years trying to repay Lucas for his kindness, but Lucas refuses to accept repayment of any kind until he is accused of shooting a white man in the back, is jailed, and in danger of being lynched. He asks Chick to examine the grave of the man he was alleged to have killed, and Chick together with a young Negro his own age, and Miss Habersham, a seventy-year-old white woman who lends her pick-up truck, set out to dig up the grave. They discover that the man in the grave is not the man Lucas is accused of killing. Eventually, it is proved that the man was not killed by Lucas, and that Lucas is the victim of chicanery. Lucas insists on paying Chick

---

[31] Jack Kerouac, *On the Road* (New York: Viking, 1957), p. 9.

for his services, but Chick has the satisfaction of knowing that he has saved Lucas' life. The work constitutes a study of what occurs when two proud, inner-directed characters try to become independent of each other, but have to admit eventually that they must depend on each other. *Intruder in the Dust* makes an excellent companionpiece to study with *The Adventures of Huckleberry Finn* because of the similarities in the Chick-Lucas and Huck-Jim relationships.

Another work of Faulkner's which the student should find engaging is *The Bear.* Faulkner has written two versions of this work—one short and simplified, the other much longer and more complex. The longer version obviously is more suitable for the brighter student. In both stories, however, we get a profound insight into the character of young Ike McCaslin, who joins his father and others every year in the hunt for the legendary Old Ben, a bear that they really do not intend to kill, but rather just to confront. Each year Ike learns more of nature, and by the time he is sixteen he can cover the entire woods without his rifle or compass. This communion with nature inspires in him qualities of courage, faith, humility, and integrity. In the longer version the bear is eventually killed in a vicious encounter because he begins to kill domesticated animals just for the sake of the kill. To the men, he has violated the code of nature in doing so. And Ike, for reasons which Faulkner elaborates on in the section on the genealogy of the families of the area, feels a sort of primal curse on the land as a result of the white man's exploitation of the Negro and the Indian, which he relates to the killing of Old Ben. His sense of guilt forces him to repudiate his patrimony and to live the simple life of a carpenter. The student can compare Ike and Huck as persons of unimpeachable integrity.

Two works in which young men go out into the world after living sheltered lives, and learn of its cruel and inhumane ways are Hawthorne's "My Kinsman, Major Molineux" and Melville's *Redburn.* In the former, a country lad, Robin, goes to a New England port city to make his way in the world with help he hopes to get from his uncle Major Molineux, a British colonial magistrate during the American Revolution. In a gripping climactic scene, which makes an effective impression on students, he sees his uncle tarred and feathered and paraded about the town in a cart while the townsfolk jeer at him. The innocent Robin is terribly disillusioned by this spectacle, and the story ends in such a way as to make it hard to determine what he plans for his future. It is certain, however, that he has incurred a psychic wound which will affect him for life. In Melville's novel, set in the mid-nine-teenth century. Redburn undergoes a similar experience. As an appren-tice seaman, he suffers unbelievable indignities in his first cruise aboard a ship making its way to Liverpool. He has to clean pigpens, and put up with the merciless teasing of the sailors. One of the seamen, Jackson, a caricaturized Claggart, provokes dreadful fear in him. He suffers home-sickness and is given to much weeping. In Liverpool he sees squalor, starvation, crime, and human degeneration to a degree he has never deemed imaginable, and his trip with his unstable and strange friend Harry to a curious institution of immorality where men gamble, use opium, and indulge in obvious perversities (implicit more than explicit) culminates his experiences. He returns to America a much different person from what he was when he left. One could compare Robin and Redburn with Nick Adams, who undergoes a similar initiation.

Young Amory Blaine, the hero of Fitzgerald's *This Side of Paradise*, is a representative youth of the 1920's. Amory is a loosely other-directed person. He has ephemeral love affairs; is flippant with his mother; and because of a lack of self-discipline does poorly in the prestigious prep school St. Regis, and later at Princeton. One detects little autobio-graphical touches of the basically other-directed Fitzgerald in this novel. This comes through in such items as Amory's becoming an alco-holic by degrees and his statement, "It's essentially cleaner to be corrupt and rich than it is to be innocent and poor."[32] In the early stages of the work Amory is gay, light-hearted, and witty. In the later stages he undergoes changes in character for which there is scanty preparation. He goes off to war, but there is little said of how the war affects him; and in his hopeless love affair with Rosalind, he suffers sudden trauma, hallucination, and severe melancholia. This poses a problem that could challenge the bright student to do a close reading of the text to deter-mine if Fitzgerald injects some subtle elements in his narrative which could account for *development* rather than *change*.

The young student is usually deeply impressed by Thomas Wolfe's *Look Homeward, Angel*. As one becomes older, however, Wolfe becomes less impressive in comparison to such authors as Faulkner, Melville, or Hawthorne. But *Look Homeward, Angel* is a valuable work as a basic document of contrasting characters as seen through the eyes of its hero Eugene Gant, who, despite Wolfe's disclaimers, is his alter ego in the

[32] Fitzgerald, p. 260.

same manner that George Willard the main character in *Winesburg, Ohio* is Sherwood Anderson's alter ego. The work is the biography of a family and the widely divergent characters that make up that family: a poetic and maudlin father; a materialistic yet tender-hearted mother; a brother who is morbidly introverted; one who is healthily extroverted; another who is cruel, vicious, and selfish; a sister with artistic talents; and so forth. In addition it is set in a boarding house where many and varied people come and go. Eugene appeals to young readers because of his complicated emotional states. He reflects their own frustrations and confusions in many ways. Like many young people, he overreacts to situations, and his emotional states are often mixed and ambivalent. He can be cruel and kind at the same time; love and hate simultaneously; be foolish one minute, then wise the next. There is a real roundness to his character. Yet, from an aesthetic standpoint, he is not so complex nor subtle a character as Huck, Holden, Ike, and some others. Wolfe's rhetoric, which has a tendency to become cloying and gushing, often causes his characterization to be overdone. His ability to create convincingly complex characters suffers because of a lack of restraint and control in his presentation. Thus, one finds him hard to reread. Since the work does encompass so many different kinds of character, however, it has great pedagogical value for introducing the student to the concept of characterization.

John Knowles' *A Separate Peace* is an interesting study in characterization. Gene Forrester and Phineas Fletcher are classmates in the same prep school during the early 1940's and very close friends. Gene is an intellectual and a good athlete; Finney a poor student but a gifted athlete. Finney has a strange psychic control over Gene. He is completely dominant. He determines what classes they will cut, where they will go, and what they will do. Gene secretly resents this, and overcompensates by putting more effort into his studies to surpass Finney. Finney is not aware of his tyranny, however, and even less aware of Gene's resentment. This leads to some strange complications. Gene begins to hate Finney violently, and is responsible for causing his awkward fall from a tree which the boys jump from daily into a creek below. This becomes a ritual for what they may have to do when they are drafted into the service. The ritual, of course, was engineered by Finney, and Gene goes along with it daily against his will. The fall causes Finney to be permanently crippled, and thus unfit for the military service for which he was so eager. Eventually, the injury causes his death. One learns by the end of the book that the difficulties between the two boys were caused by a basic lack of communication which could have been avoided had Gene resisted Finney a little more, and had Finney been a little less domineering. The real culprit is Gene, and Finney is depicted as a saintly character—innocent, naive, and thoroughly trusting of Gene; and never willing to believe that Gene deliberately causes his fall, even when Gene admits it. He exerted his authority over Gene only as an act of pure love, which to him meant sharing a unique and unusual experience with a friend. Gene, however, misinterprets him. Incidentally, in this work as in *The Adventures of Huckleberry Finn* there are no homosexual implications in the text proper. Students seldom conceive of Huck and Jim as homosexuals, and are usually surprised to learn that some critics do.

Riesman's terms of inner, other, and tradition direction, and Forster's terms of flat and round have been suggested throughout this chapter as pedagogical devices to assist the teacher and the student in classifying and interpreting character. Parallel terms for flat and round are type and individual, respectively. Expanding a little on Forster's terms, one might say that a thoroughly convincing, well-constructed character is really flat and round simultaneously. This is to suggest the Coleridgian notion that all well-conceived art consists of the universal and the particular in a coalescing unity. Applying this to characterization we see that such persons as Huck Finn, Holden Caulfield, and Henry Fleming are typical in that they represent the universal problems of youth, but individual in that they are unique, specific persons. If a character becomes too typical, he takes on allegorical and abstract qualities as Billy Budd and Claggart do in relation to Vere. If he becomes too individualized, he takes on idiosyncratic qualities as Eugene Gant does to a degree, or Emmalene Grangerford or some of the characters of Anderson's *Winesburg, Ohio* to a greater degree. Idiosyncrasy taken too far leads to caricature or grotesqueness. It is impossible for any critic or student to determine with absolute accuracy how typical or how individual a given character is, but the purpose of literary criticism is to try to do so in order to enhance understanding and appreciation. Again, both the teacher and the student must depend finally on the text of the work under study in trying to make these determinations. After this is done to the limits of one's capacities, it is then possible to rely on intuitive and impressionistic judgments in making a final judgment. For, regardless of what is in the text, one always brings his own experiences to a work, and this accounts for the wide divergencies of opinion as to what a work "really" means, and helps to make the job of interpretation more interesting and rewarding for all readers.

2

Theme

The concept of theme is crucial to an intelligent analysis and understanding of literature. To Loban, "Theme is strictly idea—the idea that
gives the literary work its roots in life, the idea that pervades and gives
universality to the action. It is the overriding truth behind the story."[1]
Theme is more than idea, however. It is idea dramatized, amplified,
and projected into high truth, a guiding, controlling root idea which
gives unity and focus to the artist's vision. In this sense, like the concept
of characterization, it is an element of content as distinguished from
style.

Theme is crucial to the development of character. Ideas are meaningless unless they relate to the human condition and take root in human
experience. The universal laws of mathematics and science would
scarcely provide suitable material for the themes of literature because
there is nothing in the operations of these laws which relates directly to
the problems of persons in real-life situations. However, the ideas
generated whenever man confronts himself, others, society, or nature
do provide the raw materials of theme. Thurston suggests that "the
central problem for the reader once the theme has been detected, is to
consider *what has happened to the theme in the process of the story*."[2] One will
ordinarily discover that the development of theme usually runs a parallel course with the development of character, and that the two developments are often indistinguishable. Thus it is often possible to teach
characterization in terms of theme, and theme in terms of characterization.

In *Story and Structure*, Laurence Perrine posits some pedagogically
sound guidelines which the teacher may employ in teaching theme:

[1] Loban, p. 327.
[2] Thurston, p. 3.

Although a theme may be partially expressed in a phrase, the student must strive to express it in an expanded sentence if he is to state it more accurately and comprehensively. For example, one would not state the theme of Faulkner's "Barn Burning" simply as father-son relationships. Rather, one would say that the theme of the story involves the tragic complications which develop when Sarty Snopes experiences the agony of having to choose between two loyalties, each of which claims his absolute allegiance: filial obedience and the demands of conscience. A theme must be a generalization about life which has universal validity, and is in the common run of experience. The problems of Willa Cather's Paul suggest themes which the young student can often relate to his own life. However, a theme ought not to undergeneralize; that is, a minor idea cannot encompass a major idea. One cannot say, for example, that a major theme of *The Adventures of Huckleberry Finn* involves Huck's associations with women. This is a minor idea which can relate to a major idea, but in a subordinate manner. A theme must be as comprehensive as possible, account for all the major details in a work, and not be contradicted by any of the details. For example, Huck's worth as a person cannot be discredited by the fact that he lies and plays pranks. In fact these details support the impression of his goodness, for he has no malicious intentions, and, indeed, often intends through deception to effect a positive good. Nor can the detail of Henry Fleming's flight in battle discredit the fact that he attains courage, if one considers the major theme of *The Red Badge of Courage* to involve the attainment of courage. A theme must not be formulated on supposed facts, but rather on the facts as presented in the work. For example, it is impossible to determine with any degree of certainty what might have happened to Billy Budd had Vere made a different decision, or what kind of a person Holden Caulfield will be when he is thirty years old. A theme ought not to be a cliche or a platitude. The student must avoid such trite and over-generalized expressions as "man's inhumanity to man" or "good versus evil" (with "good" always triumphant). It is important for the student to see that no theme can be absolutely and definitively stated. All statements of theme must be rigorously qualified, and even the qualifications must often be further qualified. The "Yes, but. . . ." qualification applies to theme as it does to any problem of literary analysis which requires explication and interpretation. No statement, ranging from a simple sentence to a volume, can replace the vision expressed by the artist in his own words. At best the statement may clarify and assist in interpretation, but at worst it may but paraphrase, or worse yet, mislead and confuse.[3]

There may be valid disagreements as to what constitutes the major theme of a work. Some works may be multi-thematic in that they suggest several or many themes, each perhaps of coordinate rank. Professional critics, as will be demonstrated throughout this discussion, are often in violent disagreement with each other in regard to theme and they frequently compete with each other fiercely in their attempts to advance original, sometimes esoteric, interpretations of theme. Yet, more must be done to make the student aware of the work of the critics. Too often, major works of literature are taught in the secondary school with no reference whatsoever to any criticism, and, as a result, students find the literature dull and meaningless. Most teachers are unable to detect the subtleties of good literature unaided. What the critics have to offer is indispensable for broadening the teacher's understanding, and their offerings are available in many inexpensive paperback casebooks and anthologies of criticism.

The concept of theme as a pedagogical unit receives much support from authorities on the teaching of English. George Hillocks, Jr., argues:

What then is the value of the thematic unit? The proponents of teaching the theme argue that there are two primary values: integration and motivation. They argue that students enjoy working with a theme and that the use of such a theme permits the integration of reading, writing, listening, and speaking activities, as well as the integration of ideas with vicarious and personal experiences. Building work around the central theme allows the student to explore the theme at his own level of interest, experience, and ability, and, at the same time to make significant contributions to the class work.[4]

The teacher may approach the theme-concept unit either deductively or inductively; that is, he may give the students a predetermined theme and have them extract from the story the details that support that theme; or he may have them determine the theme on the evidence of the details available. Perhaps it would be best to employ the inductive method as often as possible because it is less authoritarian and encourages the student to derive his own generalizations. On the other hand, the deductive method is more useful when the student is unable to draw a

---

[3] Laurence Perrine, *Story and Structure* (New York: Harcourt, Brace & World, 1959), pp. 142–44.

[4] George Hillocks, Jr., "The Theme-Concept Unit in Literature," *Patterns and Models for Teaching English* (Champaign: NCTE, 1964), p. 17.

generalization which makes sense, or has not had enough experience in analyzing literature. Burton argues a case for the deductive approach in his observation that, "Most students are interested in ideas, and a skillfully stated idea, stated as a theme for study, may serve as a real spark for student motivation."[5] In practice the teacher ought to employ both methods according to circumstance.

Thurston points out that,

There is no specific place that one need begin in analyzing a short story; usually one begins with some aspect of the story that one understands . . . and then proceeds to relate it to the other elements.[6]

The same holds true with respect to supporting or determining theme, which represent respectively the deductive and inductive approaches. One need not follow a specific order in thematic analysis, but for the less sophisticated student it would probably be better to work from the beginning to the end. In either case it is essential that the student read the work in its entirety before any attempt at thematic analysis be made. At this point the objective test can prove a most valuable device to determine whether the student is ready to proceed to more complex levels of appreciation and understanding. The student is given an objective examination to test his mastery of the literature at a basic informational level. Then, after class discussion (which can prove futile unless the student has attained an understanding at the basic level) the student should be ready to meet the more sophisticated demands of the critical paper and the essay examination.

Hayakawa observes that one of the major deficiencies of students in their language skills lies in the fact that

They go on indefinitely, reciting insignificant facts, never able to pull them together to frame a generalization that would give a meaning to the facts. Other speakers remain stuck at higher levels of abstraction, with little or no contact with lower levels. Such language remains permanently in the clouds.[7]

Through the theme-concept unit approach to the study of literature the student can develop the necessary skills of deduction and induction by which he may gain "the power of reducing multitude into unity of

[5] Burton, p. 266.

[6] Thurston, p. 2.

[7] S. I. Hayakawa, *Language in Thought and Action* (New York: Harcourt, Brace & World, 1964), p. 188.

effect and modifying a series of thoughts by some one predominant thought or feeling,"[8] and thus proceed toward a more intelligent understanding of literature. A well-formulated theme unifies the disparate elements in a work of art, and thus serves to satisfy "the universal yearning for dynamic order"[9] that all sensitive people experience.

It would seem that all the ideas contained within the works under consideration here ultimately relate to the kinds of experience each of the young heroes undergoes. Thus, in setting up a theme-concept unit the teacher may employ as his all-encompassing theme the idea of the experiential development of the young hero, who is affected in some manner by everything that occurs in the work. Like Whitman's celebrated child who went forth, the young hero becomes all that he experiences. The theme of initiation, then, becomes the standard of reference or the controlling essence through which one can observe and trace out the development of character. In effect, then—at least in the works considered here—theme and characterization can be equated to each other as coordinate elements of content.

Americans have characteristically valued the knowledge gained from first-hand experience as the most useful knowledge one could possess. Having its basis in the empirical method of John Locke, this attitude was given full expression in the eighteenth century by such writers as Benjamin Franklin and Thomas Paine, who preferred common sense over revelation and authority for determining reality and solving human problems. In the nineteenth century the transcendentalists were to give even greater dignity to this conception of experience by making of it the vehicle through which one attained self-reliance and self-realization. Later in the century the concept of experience loomed important as an element in the philosophy of pragmatism and the literature of naturalism. In the twentieth century, it provided the basis for the Imagist attitudes, and many novelists, of whom Hemingway is most representative, gave it prime treatment in their art. That the concept of experience should become an important factor in the development of American culture is natural for a growing nation with an expanding frontier, a pluralistic society, no deeply rooted past or traditions, and none of the conventional worries of the compact nations of Europe. One would expect that American literature should reflect

[8] Samuel Taylor Coleridge in Loban, p. 118.
[9] Loban, p. 619.

this attitude, and indeed it does. James Baldwin sums up the position taken by many American writers: "One writes of one thing only—one's own experience. Everything depends on how relentlessly one forces from this experience the last drop, sweet or bitter, it can possibly give."[10] And, if the writer succeeds in recreating his experience, then the reader ought to respond in the manner suggested by Thornton Wilder:

This is the way things are. I have always known it without being fully aware that I knew it. Now in the presence of this play or novel or poem . . . I know that I know it.[11]

The American conception of experience is most elaborately expressed in the writings of John Dewey, who gives a higher priority or value to *a posteriori* knowledge than to *a priori* knowledge with regard to the demands of everyday living in a democratic society. Action takes precedence over thought. But Dewey does admit that *a priori* attitudes have their place in philosophy and aesthetics; thus, one cannot accuse him of outright anti-intellectualism. In effect Dewey was interpreting the temper of his age, and keeping substantially in the same tradition as Thoreau and Emerson before him. The most reliable type of knowledge in Dewey's terms comes from what one experiences at an empirical level rather than from what he has learned through tradition, revelation, or the processes of pure thought. The doctrine of pragmatism is based on this outlook. No outcome of any human action in attempting to solve a problem or to achieve an insight can receive pragmatic sanction unless it is proved to be useful or beneficial in some way. And, one cannot prove this usefulness without submitting an action to the test of experience. Since one is not sure of an outcome before an action is taken, his relying on experience often entails risk and uncertainty. But, according to Dewey, risk must be incurred if there is to be any progress in human affairs. The attainment of knowledge in this experiential manner is summed up in the educational bromide "learning by doing." The settlement of the West and the development of the political, religious, and educational institutions unique to American culture best exemplify the pragmatic process at work.

The experiential process is truly an educative process, and all education is acquired through both first-hand experience and vicarious experience. Many of the works under consideration here could readily

[10] James Baldwin, *Notes of a Native Son* (Boston: Beacon Press, 1957), p. 7.
[11] Thornton Wilder, *Three Plays* (New York: Bantam, 1961), p. vii.

be retitled *The Education of* ————. For each of the young heroes does often come into contact with many types of experience, many changing conditions of environment to which, in Dewey's terms, he adapts as do the organisms of nature. He uses as his guidelines his past experiences which he continually reconstructs in order to make a better adaptation. One can liken this rhythm of reconstruction to what occurs when a seed is transformed into a flower through the assimilation of other elements, and thus trace the unmistakable steps through which character develops. Dewey states, "Because experience is the fulfillment of an organism in its struggles and achievements in a world of things, it is art in germ."[12]

Huck Finn is an empiricist of the first rank. He demonstrates early in the novel his distaste for anything that smacks of the authority of Sunday School, and he pokes fun at Tom Sawyer for Tom's ridiculous and slavish dependence on the so-called authorities of romantic fiction. Huck displays a remarkable ability to adapt to his environment. He is a past master at the art of reverse psychology, as he illustrates in the episode in which he wards off the bounty hunters who are on the lookout for runaway slaves, and he is adept at detecting and making good use of human selfishness, as he does with the wharf keeper whom he entices to rescue the outlaws trapped on the *Walter Scott*. He sees through the sham, pretentiousness, and brutality of all adults in a manner remarkable for a boy of his years.

Huck is eager for new experience. He confronts it head-on, often mindless of the consequences, unless someone else's safety, such as Jim's, is at stake. He profits readily from all experience, fulfilling Dewey's assertion that

the live creature adopts its past; it can make friends with even its stupidities, using them as warnings that increase present wariness. Instead of trying to live upon whatever might have been achieved in the past, it uses past successes to inform the present.[13]

Perhaps the most important influence on Huck comes from his associations with Pap, from whom he has learned how to handle difficult situations and people. This is dramatically and revealingly illustrated when he encounters the Duke and the Dauphin, a pair of outrageous frauds whom he is able to see through almost immediately. He gets

[12] Dewey, p. 19.
[13] *Ibid.*, p. 18.

along with them and keeps them at bay because he has been able to effect "a transformation of energy into thoughtful action, through assimilation of meanings from the background of past experiences."[14] In short, through Pap he has learned how to come to terms with the nightmarish aspects of reality, and the contradictions of life that few can endure; he has learned how to bend in order not to break; how to accept an experience in its entirety and come out the wiser and the more perceptive for it.

Through his day-to-day associations with Jim on the raft, Huck engages in types of experience which serve to mature him and to deepen his insights into the true nature of man. Jim serves to counterbalance the negative influences of Pap, and becomes in effect a father substitute. Lauriat Lane argues that Huck and Jim have attained the quintessential in experiential development "and have come as close as possible to the world of spirit."[15] In direct proportion as Huck immerses himself in experience his character undergoes positive development. He acquires humility and a sense of liberation from the corrupting influences of society. V. S. Pritchett views Huck's experiential development as "Movement . . . one of the great consolers of human woe; movement, a sense of continual migration, is the history of America."[16]

Experience does not rob Huck of his elemental innocence. He does not become cynical, nor does he become morbidly alienated from society as do Sal Paradise and Clyde Griffiths. He does not bear the Calvinistic stigma so typical of those who are initiated away from society by a process that R. W. B. Lewis describes as "deinitiation."[17] Huck's character develops in a direct line with the flux of experience that is his lot. It is a vital, spontaneous, variegated process of growth that occurs naturally and effortlessly in keeping with Bergson's proposition that "a really living life should never repeat itself. Wherever there is repetition or complete similarity, we suspect some mechan-

---

[14] *Ibid.*, p. 60.

[15] Lauriat Lane, Jr., "Why *Huckleberry Finn* is a Great World Novel," in Scully Bradley *et al.*, eds., *The Adventures of Huckleberry Finn*, (New York: Norton, 1962), p. 370.

[16] V. S. Pritchett, "*Huckleberry Finn* and the Cruelty of American Humor," in Bradley, *Huck Finn*, p. 307.

[17] R. W. B. Lewis, *The American Adam* (Chicago: The University of Chicago Press, 1955), p. 115.

ism at work behind the living."[18] In this sense Huck becomes a thoroughly round character through his ability to utilize experience to his own profit. He controls experience; it does not control him.

The Red Badge of Courage is a basic document on the process of a young person's, Henry Fleming's, experiential development. Hart observes correctly that

Crane's main theme is the discovery of self, that unconscious self, which, when identified with the inexhaustible energies of the group, enables man to understand the deep forces that have shaped man's destiny. The progressive movement of the hero, as in all myth, is that of separation, initiation, and return . . . he is transformed through a series of rites and revelations into a hero.[19]

Crane spells out in easily discernible details the steps through which Henry moves from fear to courage and from ignorance to enlightenment through a series of experiences that effect a continual rhythm of self-discovery and rediscovery. How appropriate to Henry's situation is Dewey's observation that "Experience is a matter of the interaction of organism with its environment, an environment that is human as well as physical, that includes the materials of tradition and institutions as well as local surroundings."[20] For Henry's life, as can be easily demonstrated by passages in the text, is significantly affected by his attitudes toward others, his uncertainties about his own worth, his observations of the indifferent and inexorable laws of nature, and the prevailing mores of his culture.

Henry is no stranger to the workings of experience with respect to the problems and uncertainties he confronts in his own life. He recalls that in his early youth on the farm he had to experiment in order to solve a problem or achieve a certainty. It is in his nature to experiment continuously. He reveals this even in his attempt to "psych-out" his comrades' thoughts to discover their own doubts and uncertainties, and in his eagerness to pass the supreme test in engaging the enemy. He is aware, too, however, that all his experimentation "involves a risk; it is a venture into the unknown, for as it assimilates the present to the

---

[18] Bergson, p. 82.

[19] John E. Hart, "*The Red Badge of Courage* as Myth and Symbol," in Scully Bradley *et al.*, eds., *The Red Badge of Courage* (New York: Norton, 1962), p. 264.

[20] Dewey, p. 246.

past it also brings about some reconstruction of that past."[21] And this risk must be incurred if there is to be any validity to Stallman's belief that

The theme of *The Red Badge of Courage* is that man's salvation lies in change. in spiritual growth. It is only by immersion in the flux of experience that man becomes disciplined and develops in character, conscience, or soul.[22]

The apex of Henry's experiential development is finally attained when, after the smoke of the battle has cleared, he finds that he is rewarded for his pains:

With the conviction came a store of assurance. He felt a quiet manhood, non-assertive, but of sturdy and strong blood. He knew that he would no more quail before his guides wherever they should point. He had been to touch the great death and found that, after all, it was but the great death. He was a man.[23]

The student must be made aware that there are touches of didacticism in this ringing declaration which tend to romanticize and give gloss to Henry's initial fear; or for that matter, depending on how one interprets Henry's actions, his cowardice.

The experiential development of Holden Caulfield presents a unique case. Unlike Huck and Henry, Holden is overpowered by experience and unequal to its demands. He seems constitutionally incapable of profiting from his past mistakes and misjudgments, and is thus unable to effect the reconstruction necessary to come to terms with his environment, and to resolve the contradictions and frustrations of his life. As a result, Holden undergoes a deterioration of personality. For "Whenever the bond that binds the living creature to his environment is broken, there is nothing that holds together the various phases and factors of the self."[24]

---

[21] *Ibid.*, p. 272.

[22] R. W. Stallman, "Notes Toward an Analysis of *The Red Badge of Courage*," in Bradley, *Red Badge*, p. 251.

[23] Stephen Crane, *The Red Badge of Courage*, ed. Richard Chase (Boston: Houghton Mifflin, 1960), p. 118.

[24] Dewey, p. 252.

In a sense, Holden is a natural Platonist. He prefers being over becoming. He distrusts the flux of experience and the instability and insecurity wrought by change. His fascination with the static objects in the city museum reveals this attitude:

The best thing, though, in that museum, was that everything stayed right where it was. Nobody'd move. You could go there a hundred thousand times and that Eskimo would still be just finished catching those two fish . . . . Nobody'd be different.[25]

Holden's passion for timeless universals is revealed in yet other ways. He knows, for example, that the quality of a good composition is not dependent on the proper placing of commas, as Stradlater believes it to be. There is in all good writing an enduring essence which transcends the mechanics of punctuation or any other accidental elements. He is obsessed with the desire to protect the innocence of the young because he knows that experience can destroy innocence. And, in his desire to isolate himself from society by living as a hermit, he makes a final desperate effort to bypass the effects of all experience. Holden and Huck differ in that Huck is willing to incur the risks involved in confronting experience; and Huck, unlike Holden, does not consciously concern himself with Platonic essences. Holden and Henry are similar in that they are both trying to achieve an ideal state of existence, but Henry does so by facing experience directly, while Holden does so by short-circuiting the obstacles and risks which experience entails.

Holden's perceptions become blunted by his efforts to curb the flux of experience. As a result he becomes further removed from the ideal state he is seeking, and increasingly loses his touch with reality. This is revealed in a minor way in his language habits. He employs incessantly such words as "goddam" and "chrissake" in a manner unrelated to their original meanings. This suggests a breach between the symbol (the word) and the reality (the meaning), which characterizes Holden's way of life. (One could argue from this that these words are not really in bad taste because they are mere ejaculations with no semantic import.) In a major way, Holden's refusal to face experience desensitizes him to the condition of others, and alienates him from the stream of sympathy and understanding so necessary for the cultivation of the virtue of charity and the development of true inner direction. Thus, Holden's refusal to confront experience and incur its risks make

[25] Salinger, p. 121.

it impossible for him to achieve the kind of fulfillment that Huck does in
his friendship with Jim, or that Henry does in his grasping the meaning
of the "subtle brotherhood of man."

Billy Budd undergoes a type of experiential development which is
completely different from that of either Huck's or Henry's, whose
experiences are acquired at an empirical level. Huck and Henry become involved with people and situations over which they exercise
some degree of control. Billy Budd, on the other hand, becomes the
passive victim of people and situations over which he is utterly unable
to exercise any significant control. Like Huck and Henry, and unlike
Holden, however, he eventually attains to a meaningful resolution,
which is foreshadowed the evening before his execution during his
secret conference with Vere, and climaxed a moment before the noose
tightens about his neck when he utters, "God bless Captain Vere." It
seems reasonable to conclude from this that he has achieved some type
of an understanding at an intuitive level, that his death eventually
effects some higher good, that he is fulfilling a role as a messiah-martyr.
Holden also reveals some messianic tendencies but, unlike Billy, he
gives no evidence of realizing them through self-immolation for some
higher cause, though he does have self-destructive tendencies. Henry
reveals some desire for martyrdom after his flight from the front lines,
but this is short-lived, for in time his rationalizations and good fortune
at the next encounter dispel this notion. Huck has the least inclination
for martyrdom. His feigned death serves a practical end—to escape
from society and Pap. He is motivated by no ideals to serve a lofty cause,
except to aid Jim. His sole purpose is to survive and to live a life free of
constraint. Nor does he, like Holden, who, after his mistreatment at the
hands of the bellhop Maurice, wish for death in order to be pitied.
Billy faces death almost happily.

Both Huck and Billy live in a world which festers in evil, but
neither are personally corrupted by it. Huck is able to profit from the
experience of observing evil at first-hand. Billy, however, is not, though
he is easily three to five years older than Huck. Melville states, "Experience is a teacher indeed, yet did Billy's years make his experience
seem small."[26] It seems that "years" is not the crucial thing in Billy's
case. He has lived aboard ship and on the waterfront long enough to

[26] Herman Melville, *Billy Budd*, in Norman Foerster, ed., *American Poetry and Prose*
(Boston: Houghton Mifflin, 1962), p. 743.

witness many abominations. Rather it is the Edenic purity of his nature that shields him from corruption. He is the prototype of pre-lapsarian man, who has not partaken of the fruit of the tree of knowledge.

The experiential development of Faulkner's Ike McCaslin progresses in both an empirical and intuitive fashion. In effect he begins at the empirical and graduates into the intuitive. In early adolescence Ike relies on sense experience to guide him in the wilderness. By the time he is sixteen he becomes a more fully accomplished woodsman and hunter than many men of the area who have devoted their entire lives to trying to unlock the secrets of the wilderness. In a mystical sense he becomes one with nature by putting away his watch, gun, and compass and living in a Thoreauvian manner. His primitivism might be compared to that of Natty Bumpo, and his expertise and natural know-how to that of Mark Twain as a river pilot, or Captain Ahab when he navigates by log and line.

Under the mentorship of Sam Fathers, Ike undergoes a process of initiation which gives him his profound insights into the mysteries of nature, and sharpens his awareness that the land is tainted by the white man's exploitation of the Negro and the Indian. The climactic moment in Ike's career occurs when he confronts Old Ben, the bear, at close range. He then realizes that his communion with nature is complete. For the two, boy and bear, meet as peers and hold each other in mutual respect.

Ike's initiation is a far more complex matter than is indicated here. Most high school students should be able to discern its outlines—the various rituals which attach to it and the crucial part Sam Fathers plays in its development. By the time Ike is fully initiated he has blossomed into the fullness of his manhood. He has attained humility, integrity, honor, and courage. The student might compare and contrast Ike's attainment with Henry Fleming's. One could reach some interesting conclusions, for example, in regard to the conception of courage. Obviously the two young men attain courage in different ways, and it does not mean quite the same thing to them. The little mongrel that charges headlong in his attack on the bear represents Henry's type of courage, achieved after the next encounter with the enemy. This type of courage is really foolhardiness, however, while Ike's courage is based on what Sam Fathers had taught him to be the difference between being scared and being afraid.

Like Huck and Henry, Ike is an empiricist. He indulges in a process of trial and error in his effort to reconstruct experience and thus discover knowledge and truth. He differs from them, however, in that his experiential development takes more time to perfect, and in that he receives much guidance from older people. Huck and Henry are more on their own; their situations are more urgent; their margins for allowable error more narrow. Ike is the most idealized of the three. Henry is portrayed most realistically. Huck lies somewhere in between. But all three are wholesome youths who engage one's admiration and sympathy. Students should find them desirable characters with whom they can readily identify.

In *Look Homeward, Angel* Eugene Gant undergoes an experiential development which is involved and complex. Wolfe employs much concrete detail in order to make the reader aware of Eugene's sensitivity to sights, sounds, and smells. In the boarding house run by his mother Eugene makes numerous contacts with a wide variety of people, and finds himself involved in many situations which add significantly to his store of experiences. Among other things he suffers the pangs of first love, takes employment in the sordid atmosphere of Norfolk Navy Yard, and later, in college, gives in to a life of utter dissipation. His career is traced in vivid detail from his prenatal days to his late teens. He reacts to experience intensely, but he does not seem to be able to profit from it as do Huck, Henry, and Ike. Thus, he never really achieves their kind of maturity. Despite this, however, there is a certain admirable quality about him. He does possess a basic sense of integrity, although it is often colored by his emotional excesses; and one tends to sympathize with him for the agonies he suffers as a developing adolescent.

The nadir in Eugene's experiential development occurs during his days in school. Possessing a poetic sensibility and a fine mind, Eugene is intellectually stifled by his incompetent though sincere teachers. He reacts to this by reading voraciously, but he does not digest this undisciplined reading. His is the tragedy of the youth who can look to no one for proper direction and guidance, and he is not inner-directed enough to become properly self-educated. Eugene's classmates are rural boys who are pragmatically oriented. They cause their teachers much embarrassment by challenging them to justify their study of the classics. The teachers, of course, are unequal to the challenge, and thus contribute to encouraging the very anti-intellectualism it is their job to remedy.

Melville's *Redburn* is the story of a tender, naive lad who acquires too much experience too fast. He compares favorably with Robin of Hawthorne's "My Kinsman, Major Molineux," who also leaves the comfort and security of a good home to make his way in the world. The world proves a bitter teacher, and both boys have to endure traumas which are an outrage to justice and a violation of their innocence. Melville is clearly aware that experience offers no immunities nor dispensations even to the very young: "Talk not of the bitterness of middle-age and after life; a boy can feel all that, and much more, when upon his young soul the mildew has fallen."[27] Both of these works deserve careful reading. They are poignant studies of adolescent disillusionment.

George Willard, the young reporter in *Winesburg, Ohio*, engages in experiences which serve to mature him and prepare him for what promises to be a rewarding future. At the end of the work he has acquired enough sophistication to perform the archetypal act of leaving the provinces and striking out on his own for the big city. His sophistication is not acquired without some pains, however. A perceptive, sensitive person, George is eager to know of others, and he has a gift for gaining the confidence of others. He gets involved in situations with people which often cause him great embarrassment and discomfort—even personal danger; but, like the young heroes who know how to profit from their experiences, he becomes truly educated in the ways of the world. Unlike many of the grotesque, twisted characters of the novel, George has a capacity for learning which broadens his outlooks and gives him a sense of tolerance toward others.

One of George's weaknesses is that he has a tendency to become enamored with words and to confuse them with the realities for which they stand. Kate Swift, his former English teacher, sees this failing of his and advises him: "You must not become a mere peddler of words. The thing to learn is to know what people are thinking about, not what they say."[28] After a beating by the local bartender, Ed Handby, for having designs on Ed's girl, Belle Carpenter, George comes a step closer to realizing Kate's advice. Prior to the beating he had talked himself into believing that Belle was interested in him on the basis of things she said to him. He learns the hard way that words are unreliable indicators of reality.

[27] Herman Melville, *Redburn* (Garden City: Doubleday, 1957), p. 9.
[28] Sherwood Anderson, *Winesburg, Ohio* (New York: Viking, 1964), p. 163.

The apex of George's experiential development occurs just before he leaves Winesburg. He spends several hours one evening with Helen White, the banker's daughter. They scamper around happily in the dark woods like frisky pups, but have no desire for a sexual relationship. His being able to experience contentment and delight at a nonsexual level gives George a sense of self-mastery that he has never before known. He conceives of himself as a fully developed man, and armed with this insight he sets out with determination and conviction to confront new experience.

Up to the time that he is jailed for the murder of Roberta Alden, Clyde Griffiths' experiential development progresses only at the level of animal comfort. As he becomes more aware of the higher social stations in life, his appetite for social advancement and preferment increases until it becomes a ruling passion, and his moral and spiritual worth decrease in inverse proportion. By the time that he decides to murder Roberta he has become a monstrously egoistic person—unconscionable, self-indulgent, and entirely insensitive to the rights and feelings of others. Except for Studs Lonigan, he stands at this point in his career in sharp contrast to the other young heroes considered thus far v .th respect to personal integrity, humility, and selflessness. One cannot make allowances for Clyde solely on the grounds of environmental influences, nor on Dreiser's theory of "chemisms," mysterious organic forces which determine one's behavior. He is as responsible and as perceptive as Huck Finn or Ike McCaslin, but he is lacking in their ability to control and order experience in a moral way to fulfil a higher end than the mere realization of personal comfort. He is completely incapable of reconstructing past experience in any positive way. He profits from none of his mistakes. After he allows Roberta to drown, he seems to be overcome with pangs of guilt and shame. These reactions are really symptoms, however, of his fear of exposure and consequent disgrace and punishment. Moreover, during his trial he clings stubbornly and shamelessly to the story that his attorney has fabricated for him. Even after his "spiritual conversion" at the hands of the young minister in the penitentiary, there is no real evidence that Clyde is truly repentant for his actions. Rather he seems to submit to the services of the minister more out of regret and futility than contrition. He does so in desperation, for he has no other alternative if he is to preserve his emotional balance. At this point the student would do well to evaluate Clyde's "guilt" in the context of the guilt experiences some of the other young heroes undergo. The student might examine, too, the guilt responses of characters in related literature. Dimmesdale in *The Scarlet Letter* provides an excellent example.

David Stevenson observes that a new type of hero has emerged in American fiction within the past generation. He is the activist hero who is "involved in a more nearly aimless search through the endless clutter of everyday existence for a sense of a privately satisfying identity or self."[29] Sal Paradise exemplifies this type. His experiential development occurs through the medium of bars, bitches, and bus stops. A thoroughly immoral and amoral person, Sal desires experience for its own sake. His god is George Shearing, the jazz pianist whose music enraptures him into oblivion. Sal exists at a nonintellectual level. He asks no big questions; he does not concern himself with the future. Through an overdose of emotional experience he hopes to attain complete unconsciousness, as the French poet Rimbaud did. Flux, change, and instability characterize his way of life. He lives wholly for the next unknown moment, and prefers an intense, ephemeral experience to an enduring one. The contradictions and inconsistencies of life do not unsettle him as they do Holden. Thus, he is able to come to terms with his environment, and to sustain himself in a way that Holden never could.

In Sal's favor one has to say that he does have a certain, though unconventional, integrity about him. Unlike Clyde Griffiths, he is not deceived by the false values of society. In fact, he actively rejects them. He is not consciously cruel, and he is fiercely loyal to his friends. In many ways Augie March is similar to Sal in his starvation for experience. But Augie is too shackled to bourgeois values to be completely like him. *On the Road* is a basic document on the Beatnik outlook.

Perhaps the writer who has spoken most effectively in his fiction on the primacy of first-hand experience as against vicarious experience is Ernest Hemingway. Rhav observes,

There is nothing Hemingway dislikes more than experience of a make-believe, vague, or frigid nature, but in order to safeguard himself against the counterfeit, he consistently avoids drawing upon the more abstract resources of the mind, he snubs the thinking man, and mostly confines himself to the depiction of life on its physical levels.[30]

[29] David L. Stevenson, "The Activists," *Daedalus* (Spring, 1963), p. 240.
[30] Philip Rahv, *Image and Idea* (New York: New Directions, 1949), in Aldridge, p. 234.

This attitude is dramatized in most of the Nick Adams stories, and in some of the novels. Each of the short stories is in fact a compact, intense portrayal of a significant experience—usually involving death, violence, or sex—that Nick Adams undergoes and that adds to his education.

In "The Killers" Nick has a traumatic rendezvous with evil. After learning the two hired killers are in town to murder Ole Andreson, a has-been prizefighter, Nick, unlike the more sophisticated and less humane adults about him, sets out in a panic to warn the man, but to no avail. The man is tired of running and resigns himself to his fate. As Henry Fleming learns of the indifference of nature to his misfortune, so does Nick Adams learn of the indifference of the human race to the plight of its less fortunate members. The student can compare Nick's responses to those of Redburn, who, while in Liverpool, has to stand helplessly by as a mother and her two children starve to death before his eyes. The people of Liverpool display the same indifference as do those in the mid-western town where Nick Adams lives.

Two other stories in which Nick suffers trauma are "Indian Camp" and "The Battler." In the former he witnesses a Caesarian operation performed by his father with a jackknife on an Indian woman who is having difficulties with her delivery. While she is screaming, her husband, who is in the bunk above her, cuts his throat from ear to ear without a sound. The sight of this deeply affects Nick and prompts him to question his father about why people commit suicide. His father cannot give him a satisfactory answer. In the latter story he is on the road. After being beaten by a detective for trespassing on railroad property, Nick joins company with a punch-drunk ex-fighter and his companion, a Negro with a criminal record for assault with a knife. The Negro is very polite to Nick, feeds him, and protects him from the fighter, who gradually develops a strange animosity towards Nick. It is obvious that this animosity is a result of the jealousy that the fighter feels toward Nick because of the Negro's attentions to him, and this in turn suggests that the two men have an abnormal attachment to each other, which is by all indications homosexual. Each of these stories is a masterpiece of nightmare and horror. Like Poe, Hemingway creates one overpowering central impression in his short fiction, but he does so in restrained and muted language. Ordinarily, one has to read these stories several times to appreciate their full impact.

Robert Penn Warren states, "In fact Hemingway is anti-intellectual, and has a great contempt for any type of solution arrived at without the immediate testings of experience. . . . The careful relish of sen-
sation—that is what counts always."[31] In none of Hemingway's works,
perhaps, is this attitude better exemplified than in "Big Two-Hearted
River." On the surface this story concerns itself with a camping trip
which Hemingway describes with clinical objectivity. Nick Adams
performs an elaborate ritual in pitching his tent, starting a camp fire,
and preparing his food. All of his senses are engaged in what he is doing.
His hunger is described at length; his reactions to cold water; his savor-
ing the smoke of his cigarette. In addition, Hemingway takes extended
pains to describe the concrete imagery of nature—the sun, the grass-
hoppers, the soil, the plant life. Then, in what amounts almost to an
epic action, Nick meticulously places his bait on a fishhook and casts
a line into the river. There are only two occasions on which Nick has
any thoughts which are not the result of concrete, sensory experience.
One occurs when he thinks of his playboy friend Hopkins, the Texas
millionaire; the other when he becomes frightened as the river courses
into a dark, shaded swamp area. In each case he blanks these thoughts
from his mind and makes a concerted effort to get back to the pure
experiences of the senses, which is obviously the only kind of experience
he desires.

It is unfortunate that some high-school anthologies contain this
story in isolation. To understand it properly the student must study it in
context with other Nick Adams stories. Otherwise it will not make
much sense. The student may find it a tedious elaboration on a trivial
human activity, a tempest in a teapot. However, if the student knows
that Nick Adams is recovering from the effects of his experiences in the
war, and must indulge in pure sense experience as a form of therapy,
then the story will make more sense. In short, the student must see that
there is a veiled undertone of tragedy in the story.

If one had to sum up Emerson's philosophy in a categorical im-
perative, it could well be "Live, don't think!" Certainly Emerson did
believe in the infallibility of intuition, but intuition based initially on
first-hand experience, not on mysticism. Emerson saw man as a "god
in ruins," who, if he would but take the initiative and "live" could
regenerate himself by reconstructing his experience in unique and

[31] Robert Penn Warren, "Hemingway," *Kenyon Review*, IX (Winter, 1947), in Aldridge,
pp. 456–57.

original ways. In a sense Emerson is as fiercely anti-intellectual as Hemingway. Though he concedes that the thoughts of men as recorded in books can serve to inspire, he violently rejects the notion that partaking of these thoughts is a desirable end in itself. In fact he almost rejects all thought as not worthwhile, and counsels men to risk contradiction and inconsistency. The important thing is action and the risk involved in taking that action. Thought is of value only insofar as it serves as a handmaiden to action. One sees in this outlook some elements of Dewey's conception of experience.

Most of the young heroes whose experiential developments have been consistent with the Deweyan and Emersonian conceptions of experience have achieved some type of a meaningful fulfillment in their lives. Huck Finn and Ike McCaslin are intelligent and sensitive boys, but not given to book learning. They are at their happiest when they make close contact with nature—Huck on the raft, Ike in the wilderness. Thought proves an enemy to Holden Caulfield, Henry Fleming, and Martin Eden. Holden pursues thought and ends up in a sanitarium. Henry rejects thought, takes to action, and becomes a hero. Martin is most happy when he is engaged in waterfront brawls or working eighteen hours a day in a laundry. Books prove his undoing, as elemental experience proves a balm to Nick Adams' psychic wounds. Billy Budd achieves a sort of salvation through his act of faith in Captain Vere. He is probably the least intellectually inclined of all the young heroes. Studs Lonigan and Clyde Griffiths are neither thinkers nor initiators of actions which can develop and dignify their characters.

The teacher might use Hemingway's concept of the "separate peace" as a pedagogical device to illustrate how the youthful hero comes to terms with experience. The term is coined as a result of Nick Adams deciding to terminate his tour of duty in the army after receiving serious wounds and becoming disillusioned. Frederick Henry of *A Farewell to Arms* does similarly by deserting, and Jake Barnes of *The Sun Also Rises* effects his separate peace by resigning himself to his sexual impotence. In John Knowles' *A Separate Peace* it is ambiguous whether Gene Forrester resolves his guilt toward Finney. There is a distinct impression, however, that time serves to attenuate his guilt. Huck Finn makes his separate peace by lighting out for the territory, Ike McCaslin by becoming a carpenter and rejecting his patrimony, and George Willard by leaving Winesburg. Clyde, Studs, and Martin fail to achieve any kind of peace except in death, and Eugene Gant and Holden Caulfield achieve only partial peace. Melville's Ishmael makes his separate peace by striking a happy balance in his own life between Emerson's extreme transcendentalism and Ahab's transcendentalism in reverse.

The concept of the experiential development of the young hero ought to provide the teacher with an idea comprehensive enough to fulfil the pedagogical needs of the theme-concept unit referred to earlier. At the same time it ought not to be so overgeneralized as to be tenuous. It would seem that all the ideas in the works under consideration here relate somehow to this concept as spokes to a hub, and that both teacher and student have in it a workable device which can facilitate an intelligent study of literature. Consideration will now be given to the elements of style through which the author develops and presents content.

The teaching of style

3

Symbolism as style

Reduced to its lowest terms, a symbol may be defined as something that represents something else, but is not in reality the equivalent of that something else, except when made so by one's imagination. In order to re-create and communicate experience, it is essential that human beings have at their disposal convenient symbols, accessible to the senses, and standardized to a degree that will permit a consensus among a given group of people with respect to the kinds of experience the symbols represent.

Essentially, the sum total of one's experiences is the sum total of what one knows, and knowledge, as suggested earlier, may be acquired either *a priori* or *a posteriori* through the mind and the senses respectively. An empiricist, though not denying the reality of *a priori* knowledge, would give a higher value to *a posteriori* knowledge, and a rationalist would do the converse. In this discussion no such bias will be held. Each of the modes of acquiring knowledge will be accorded equal rank and viewed as complementary and supplementary to each other.

As a result of engaging in thought and action, one acquires intuitive knowledge, which is not really *a priori* or *a posteriori* knowledge, but rather a synthesis of both. Some characters seem to have intrinsic intuitive insight, not dependent upon prior knowledge or experience. Billy Budd would exemplify this type most effectively. Most of the other young heroes, however, acquire intuitive insights in the course of their experiential developments. The ultimate in intuitive knowledge is usually achieved in the experiences of gifted artists, scholars, and men of affairs.

Except for those who are blind or deaf, the senses of taste, smell, and touch are less important than sight and hearing for the successful acquisition of complex knowledge. It would follow, then, that if knowledge could be represented by an intelligible system of standardized signals based on sight and hearing, one would have at his disposal an instrument through which knowledge could be conveniently recreated and communicated. This instrument, of course, is language—which may be simply defined as the system through which human beings symbolize knowledge.

Perhaps the best way to teach the young student the conception of symbolism as a function of style is through a study of the symbolic processes of language. Modern linguists have asserted that language is basically speech; that is, through the breath stream working in conjunction with the tongue and various parts of the mouth and throat, human beings can produce many different specific sounds consisting of consonants, vowels, and diphthongs, which in turn can be combined in virtually an infinite variety of ways to produce unique clusters of sound. Language develops as these clusters are combined in unique ways to represent ideas. But sounds are perishable. They can be sustained no longer than one's breath. And as soon as sounds are lost, that for which they stand, ideas, are lost, and thus communicable knowledge is lost. The best way known to man (short of a tape recorder) to preserve sounds at a symbolic level is through the twenty-six characters of the alphabet, which combine in various patterns to produce the more than one-half-million words of the English language. Thus does a visual symbol preserve an aural symbol. One can summarize this involved symbolic process of language as follows: writing symbolizes sounds which symbolize ideas which result from empirical, rational, or intuitive knowledge. And, in this way language makes it possible to preserve and communicate knowledge acquired through the senses of sight and hearing.

All words, then, written or spoken, are symbols for ideas. Not all words are equal in their capacities to carry ideational content, however, for some words carry more meaning than others. The terms *denotation* and *connotation* are used to describe this phenomenon. Words with restricted meanings are denotative; words with expanded meanings are connotative. The teacher could illustrate the concepts of denotation and connotation, for example, through the color *red*. A physicist would assign a restricted meaning to the concept of redness. He would describe it as a range of colors in the radio frequency spectrum which is marked off by a certain measurable wavelength. All other physicists in the world would substantially agree with this description;

there would be little room for deviation from this established definition. The poet, on the other hand, would be able to extract more expansive meanings from the concept of redness. He may employ redness in his imagery to suggest heat, violence, passion, danger, even Communism. Individuals may respond differently to red imagery. Some may find it pleasing, others distasteful, for no other reason than subjective impressions. The physicist would find the poetic approach useless in trying to develop a scientific definition of color.

The concepts of denotation and connotation lend themselves aptly to an analogy which can be drawn from the discipline of physics: Denotation is centripetal by nature; meanings tend to concentrate centrally in a limited orbit. Connotation, on the other hand, is centrifugal; meanings tend to work out from the center in an expanding orbit.

Theoretically, pure prose is denotative and pure poetry is connotative. In practice, however, such a classification is inaccurate, for no language can be either purely denotative or purely connotative. Yet one could safely generalize that poetic expression is more connotative or more symbolic than prosaic expression. Often, this is a difficult notion for students to grasp. Many students believe that the sole criteria by which poetry is distinguished from prose are rhyme and rhythm. They fail to see that poetry may be distinguished from prose, too, by other criteria which are related to connotation. The language of poetry is likely to be quaint or archaic, ambiguous, sensuous, and picturesque. The syntax of poetry is likely to be unconventional; poetry ordinarily employs a less conversational style than prose; the poet gives more attention to prosody than does the writer of prose. One could illustrate these criteria by having the student contrast a cooking recipe or a paragraph from a law book with a poem. The contrast should prove revealing. It is often said that the language of poetry is more carefully selected and arranged than the language of prose, and that each word in a poem is more essential to the total meaning of the poem than is each word in a prose piece, but this is not necessarily true. Again, one could illustrate with a recipe or a legal statement how indispensable each word of prose could be to meaning.

If the student can discern intelligently the connotative aspects of language, he ought then to be able to interpret symbols intelligently. It seems that the interpretation of symbols is virtually nothing more than the perceptive discernment of connotations. Often, as will be illustrated later, objects, actions, and situations in literature carry connotations, and thus serve effectively as symbols. These particulars of object, action, and situation, in turn, are symbolized by the visual signals of language which the student must decode properly if he is to extract in its fullness the experience that the artist is attempting to share. In this sense a good critic is really nothing more than a skilful decoder of language, or more simply—a good reader.

Like themes, symbols must carry meanings which are rooted in universal human experience and somehow relate to the human condition. Since an artist can get more meaning out of language through the connotations of symbols, symbolism may be viewed as an alternative method that he has at his disposal to illuminate and sustain theme, and thus does symbolism truly function as an element of style. The symbol serves to render theme more accessible; to provide the reader with a special tool which can facilitate an intelligent critical analysis of literature.

There are yet other means that the teacher may employ to heighten the student's awareness of the importance of the symbolic processes. So much of human experience depends upon symbols to facilitate the conduct of human affairs. The flag symbolizes an entire nation. Money symbolizes purchasing power. A driver's license symbolizes the state's approval of a citizen's credential's to operate a motor vehicle. The phenomena of nature have symbolic significance. A storm may symbolize human passion; water often symbolizes life and regeneration; certain animals symbolize various qualities: tigers—grace, speed, coordination, and stealth; lions—power and majesty; horses—virility and nobility; foxes—cunning; and lambs—meekness, to mention a few. A grade on a report card is supposed to symbolize a student's progress in a course. Students should be able to list many more.

Whatever one's interpretation of a symbol, it must be anchored firmly to the facts of the work under study, and must somehow fit in reasonably with what the artist is attempting to express. Reasonable interpretation is often a difficult task, however. Perrine tells us that a symbol is "something that means more than what it is,"[1] and that "its richness and its difficulty result from its imprecision."[2] Symbols, by their very nature, have to be somewhat elusive; and extremely complex symbols are often so inpenetrable as to be scarcely interpretable.

[1] Laurence Perrine, *Sound and Sense* (New York: Harcourt, Brace & World, 1963), p. 69.
[2] *Ibid.*, p. 71.

One often seems on the verge of grasping their meanings but never quite does so. Kafka and Joyce write in this way because "An artistic writer does not insult his reader by telling too much."[3]

There is always the danger—especially with the superior student—that symbols may be overinterpreted, that the student may glean more meaning from the symbol than the symbol justifies. The teacher must try to be as charitable as possible in such situations. Many leading critics (Chase, Stallman, and Fiedler to name a few) seem not to be completely free from this failing, and there is often enough truth in the ambitious student's interpretation to merit some consideration. Indeed, the teacher with some reservations should encourage the student in these attempts. For often the student "dares to be himself; he dares to use his initiative; he does not require prodding. Even his occasional failures are magnificent failures; like the late Babe Ruth he strikes out with a mighty swing."[4]

The word *symbol* has been used up to this point to mean something that stands for something else, and since we are concerned with literature, all of our symbols have to consist of the substance of language, namely words. In order to be consistent with the conventional nomenclature of literary criticism, however, it is necessary to give a more specialized definition to the concept of symbolism. Often in teaching situations one has to employ this procedure; that is, to begin with a term that is used loosely, but is pedagogically appropriate because of its simplicity, and then, after the student grasps the basic material that the term clarifies, to use it more accurately. Instead of calling written words symbols (which they certainly are) it is more accurate to call them figures of speech in a restricted sense (the word "figure" being a synonym of sorts for symbol). All written words are in fact figures of speech because one cannot hear letters or see sounds. Two entirely different sense experiences are involved in writing and speaking. The spoken word, of course, is not a figure of speech because it *is* speech. Those figures of speech which are devoid of connotation do not concern us here because of their limited ability to convey expanded meanings. They are more properly placed in the province of prose. Those figures of speech that do convey expanded meanings through connotation are conveniently labeled by the familar terms *simile* and *metaphor*. A simile

[3] Hook, p. 102.
[4] *Ibid.*, p. 75.

is a figure of speech that makes an expressed comparison between two dissimilar entities through the prepositional function words "like" or "as." For example, in the statement, "He jumped from the ledge like a cat" a man and a cat are being associated in such a way that swiftness of movement is linguistically abstracted from the cat and transferred to the man. The comparison is expressed because "cat" is explicity stated. A metaphor, on the other hand, is an implied comparison. In the statement, "He sprang from the ledge" the verb "sprang" suggests the swiftness of a cat; the comparison is implicit. The statement, "He jumped from the ledge" is neither a simile nor a metaphor, and thus is devoid of connotation. The simile and the metaphor create the same connotative effects, but in different ways. In each case the concrete (man) and the abstract (swiftness) are fused, and as a result meaning is dramatically expanded and vitalized. But, since men really are not cats, a metaphor and a simile are grammatical fictions. Unless one is willing to suspend disbelief and permit imagination to equate dissimilar entities, he cannot enter into the experience that the figures of speech are designed to convey.

Metaphors and similes are of two types: symbol and allegory. The more specialized definition of symbol is given by Perrine: "Meanings ray out from a symbol like the corona around the sun, or like connotations around a richly suggested word."[5] In allegory, on the other hand, "Meanings do not ray out as from the symbol," there is, rather, "a one-to-one correspondence between its details and a set of ulterior meanings."[6] In short, a symbol has multi-dimensional meanings; allegory, a uni-dimensional meaning. Pure allegory is hard to achieve in practice. In the literature of the young hero few real allegorical figures of speech are encountered. In works like Orwell's *Animal Farm* and Hawthorne's *"Celestial Railroad"* more nearly pure allegorical figures are encountered. Our concern here will, for the most part, be with metaphors of symbol.

As symbols are often overinterpreted, so, too, are they often underestimated as legitimate devices of style. In the former instance one assigns more meaning to a symbol than is justified; in the latter, one does not extract enough meaning to appreciate the full impact of the content the symbol is supposed to convey. George Winchester Stone criticizes those who would not give a symbol its proper due:

[5] Perrine, *Sound and Sense*, p. 75.
[6] *Ibid.*, p. 77.

Metaphor is variously taught in both reading and writing as an ornament to style, as a ruse that makes the meaning more vivid or picturesque, or that gives the mind of the reader pleasing images. There is little recognition of the fact that metaphor, far from being simply a clarifier or ornament attached to the sense, is the meaning itself.[7]

Saul Bellow criticizes both extremes in a more balanced statement:

A true symbol is substantial not accidental. You cannot avoid it, you cannot remove it. You can't take the handkerchief from *Othello*. . . . You can, however, read *Ulysses* without suspecting that wood shavings have to do with the Crucifixion or that the name Simon refers to the sin of Simony. . . . These are purely peripheral matters; fringe benefits if you like.[8]

The remainder of this chapter will concern itself with the significant symbols in the literature of the young hero, and how these symbols are related to content.

Both T. S. Eliot and Lionel Trilling see the Mississippi River as the most crucial symbol in *The Adventures of Huckleberry Finn*.[9] To them the river takes on divine proportions as a sort of pagan god of nature served by Huck and Jim, who constitute a community of saints in microcosm. Jim and Huck gain peace and security when on the river. It is their avenue of escape from the evils of civilization. The river is also treacherous and ambiguous, however; it is a sewer as well as an oasis. It is the waterway, too, of the bounty-hunter and the steamboat crews, who, mindless of human life, make a sport of ramming small craft head-on. And to those who do not know the river, its sandbars and litter can mean sudden death.

To Bernard De Voto "Huck and the river's motion give continuity to a series of episodes which are in essence only developed anecdotes."[10] In this sense the river serves as the vehicle of Huck's experiential development. In a larger sense De Voto sees "the heritage of a nation not unjustly symbolized by the river's flow."[11] This last observation suggests

---

[7] Stone, p. 29.

[8] Saul Bellow, "Deep Readers of the World, Beware!" *New York Times Book Review*, February 15, 1959, p. 1.

[9] T. S. Eliot, "Introduction to *Huck Finn*," and Lionel Trilling, "The Greatness of *Huck Finn*," in Bradley, *Huck Finn*, pp. 310–28.

[10] Bernard De Voto, *Mark Twain's America* Boston: (Houghton Mifflin, 1932), in Bradley, *Huck Finn*, p. 292.

[11] *Ibid.*, p. 296–97.

that the American nation itself undergoes a kind of experiential development similar to that undergone by some of the youthful heroes of American literature. Such a contention, of course, is consistent with the facts of American history.

To Richard P. Adams, Huck's symbolic death when he escapes from the cabin where Pap is holding him like a caged animal, is the most crucial symbolic situation in the work. For it gives Huck the kind of freedom he needs to regenerate himself.[12] In fact there is a distinct pattern of symbolic deaths and rebirths throughout the work. He "dies" again after the Grangerford-Shepherdson feud, and takes to the river only to become involved with the Duke and the Dauphin. His next "death" occurs when he escapes from the digging party at the grave of Peter Wilks; and again in his role as Tom Sawyer at the Phelps farm. Each of these "deaths" leads to a rebirth of sorts through which he gains experience and knowledge. He seems to achieve a final rebirth at the novel's close when he learns of Pap's death and of Jim's being legally freed. He does not really, however, because his lighting out for the territory culminates the pattern of symbolic deaths and foreshadows yet another rebirth.

There are in *The Adventures of Huckleberry Finn* many lesser symbols of object and action which have thematic significance. Human tears usually signal the most shameless type of fraud and chicanery. One observes this when Pap weeps after resolving to reform his life, and when the Dauphin weeps so convincingly as he feigns grief over the death of Peter Wilks. When the Negroes weep, however, over the breakup of their families, their tears are genuine. Jim's five-cent piece, which he was supposed to have received from witches, is a status symbol in the Negro community. The Shepherdsons and Grangerfords symbolize the twisted Southern notion of chivalry; the Duke's forty-dollar sale of Jim symbolizes Judas' sell-out of Christ. And the townsfolk themselves—selfish, gullible, and brutal—symbolize the seamier side of human nature. In fact, one could argue that the common townfolk are the real villains of the work. The blameworthiness of the Duke and the Dauphin is extenuated because their evil is provoked by the intrinsic stupidity and greed of their victims.

[12] R. P. Adams, "The Unity and Coherence of *Huckleberry Finn*," in Bradley, *Huck Finn*, p. 344.

The Catcher in the Rye abounds in symbols which serve substantially to clarify and sustain theme. The sham, pretense, and false values of American society are symbolized by Hollywood, the producer of the twentieth-century version of bread and circuses for the people. Allie's baseball mitt, of which Holden makes a fetish, symbolizes Allie's continued influence over Holden despite his death, and Holden's incapacity to accept the reality of death. The ducks that leave for warmer climates in the winter symbolize Holden's quest for security and stability, as do the still-life objects in the museum where time is obliterated by the fantasy of an eternal now. His sister Phoebe symbolizes stability and calm. Through her, Holden achieves at least a temporary Nirvana. Mr. Spencer symbolizes decay, stagnation, and conscious cruelty; Mr. Antolini, disillusionment and betrayal; his mother and father, decadence and insensitivity. The catcher in the rye is a figment of Holden's imagination which results from his confusing the word "catch" with the word "meet" in a line from the popular folk song "Coming through the Rye." As the catcher, Holden envisions himself as a messiah who has come to save and protect the weak and the innocent.

Holden's preoccupation with sex is symbolized by the image of the violin, which he associates with the female body. The violin player represents the male sex partner, and the skillful playing of the violin is equated to the fulfillment of the sex act. As a rhetorical device the violin image is as effective as the conceits of metaphysical poetry. There are other symbols in *The Catcher in the Rye* which will be treated later in another connection.

The Red Badge of Courage is replete with the kinds of symbol one ordinarily associates with Imagist poetry. Crane's imagery is unique. It is somewhat similar to the conceits of metaphysical poetry, though not always so startling in its rhetorical effects. Like T. S. Eliot's objective correlative, it is the kind of imagery that forcefully engages the senses as well as the emotions and intellect.

Crane employs many images from nature, which he depicts as indifferent to man's plight. In this regard he differs from Emerson, who sees nature as a beneficent force, and from Melville, who sees nature as basically evil. In effect Crane views nature as an amoral force regulated by the inexorable laws of necessity and instinct. However, he does not apply this belief to the human situation, though he does admit that man's capacity for moral freedom is limited by nature. Erin and

Mordecai Marcus, who have made a detailed study of Crane's animal imagery, seem to be correct in their conclusion that "Crane still communicates the idea that it is as bad to kill like a beast as it is to run like a rabbit. Thus Crane's animal imagery contributes to his moral judgment of war."[13] And, since war is caused by man, the final judgment lies ultimately with him. The squirrel that is frightened when Henry throws a pine cone at it symbolizes the force of the instinct of self-preservation, and the tranquility of the summer day in the forest symbolizes the utter indifference of nature to the concerns of men at war. (Crane treats of these aspects of nature even more dramatically in his symbol-laden short story "The Open Boat," which the student may read in conjunction with *The Red Badge of Courage*).

Crane depicts the moving army in variegated imagery. First, it is a monster: "A moment later the regiment went swinging off into the darkness. It was now like one of those moving monsters wending with many feet."[14] Then, employing the diverse imagery of law, sociology, metallurgy, and, geometry, he says: "It [the regiment] enclosed him. And there were iron laws of tradition and law on four sides. He was in a moving box."[15] When the army is not on the move, Crane employs images which connote inertia. Henry is exasperated with the "intolerable slowness" of the generals who "seemed content to perch tranquilly on the river bank,"[16] much in the manner of Edmund Burke's whale, which, stranded on the sea shores, suggests the condition of Spain in the eighteenth century.[17] The student might be asked to compare and contrast Crane's use of the battlefield to Melville's use of the ship (in either *Billy Budd* or *Moby Dick*) as symbols which relate importantly to theme. Each symbol provides the setting, of course, in which high drama is enacted, resounding resolution achieved, and an important statement on the nature of man is made.

There are yet other symbols which Crane employs to good effect. The flag which Henry wrenches from a dead Confederate soldier is represented as a goddess maiden that must be won, and the possession of it relates to Crane's earlier comment that the soldiers are motivated

---

[13] Erin and Mordecai Marcus, "Animal Imagery in *The Red Badge of Courage*," in Bradley, *Red Badge*, p. 312.

[14] Crane, p. 14.

[15] *Ibid.*, p. 21.

[16] *Ibid.*, p. 13.

[17] Herman Melville, *Moby Dick* (New York: Bobbs-Merrill 1964), p. 16.

to fight in order to gain the favor of women. John E. Hart sees blood as a crucial image: "Just as in the rites of some primitive tribes or as in Christ's crucifixion on the cross, 'blood' plays an essential part in the act of atonement and in the process of transformation."[18] And, of course, Henry's wound is a central image. Acquired by accident, it serves to make Henry a hero to his comrades, but secretly it is his badge of shame. It becomes a psychic wound of sorts which gnaws away at him. Yet he gains from it the instinctual courage he needs to redeem his shame. Nick Adams, Ike McCaslin, and Holden Caulfield never fully achieve Henry's kind of resolution. He is probably the most triumphant of all the young heroes in that he controls his experience most satisfactorily.

The Red Badge of Courage is replete with concrete images that give real substance to otherwise vague abstraction. The following passage will illustrate:

Once the line encountered the body of a dead soldier. He lay upon his back staring at the sky. He was dressed in an awkward suit of yellowish brown. The youth could see that the soles of his shoes had been worn to the thinness of writing paper, and from a great rent in one the dead foot projected piteously. And it was as if fate had betrayed the soldier. In death it exposed to his enemies that poverty which perhaps in life he had concealed from his friends.[19]

Such a passage is most effective rhetorically. It engages all the senses, and fulfills all the criteria of the objective correlative. It employs a few well-chosen words whose connotations "ray out" to create a complete picture, and achieves the kind of excellence in writing that Hemingway suggests through his analogy of the iceberg, the one-eighth of which above the surface that should bring to mind the seven-eights which lies submerged out of sight. Later in this chapter more will be said in regard to the symbolism in *The Red Badge of Courage*.

Of all the works under consideration here *Billy Budd* comes the closest to allegory. Unlike the whale, Moby Dick, which is a true symbol because of the multiplicity of meanings it suggests, the characters Billy Budd and Claggart approach more the one-to-one ratio which characterizes true allegory. They would represent, respectively, good and evil. But, in fact, as has been suggested earlier, each is neither absolutely good nor evil. Billy has some flaws, such as his quick temper,

[18] Hart, "*Red Badge* as Myth and Symbol," in Bradley, *Red Badge*, p. 268.
[19] Crane, p. 22.

his inability to profit from experience, and his unadmirable passivity in the face of outrageous injustive. Claggart has some virtues in his efficiency, his dedication to duty, and his natural qualities of leadership. But, in relation to Vere, they are, of course, less individualized and thus more allegorical. Yet in another sense all three men are truly symbolic characters of coordinate rank aesthetically. Billy Budd's situation is analogous to that of Christ, Adam, or Isaac; Vere's to Pilate, God the Father, or Abraham; and Claggart's to the Serpent of Eden. Or one might interpet them more generally: Claggart might represent that element in mankind which cannot endure virtue and innocence, and Billy Budd that element which accepts virtue and innocence as the highest good. Vere would then represent a kind of Everyman, a synthesis of this duality. As a public servant Vere would have to allow that evil must be permitted, although his personal feelings would incline to the side of virtue and innocence.

Billy Budd and Claggart are in many ways pawns in the hands of fate. Their actions often seem uncontrolled by reason. They seem to act as they do because they are constitutionally incapable of doing otherwise. Thus do they symbolize the mysteries of the workings of fate. Vere, on the other hand, is capable of thought and reflection; his actions are controlled by reason; he is sensitive to the demands of justice, and well schooled in the realities of the human situation. Thus does he symbolize the power of will, and the sorrows men must endure when they are called upon to pass ultimate judgments in human affairs. Phil Withim sees ambiguities in Vere. Ordinarily, Vere is interpreted to mean "truth" from the Latin "veritas." Withim suggests, however, that Vere might also mean "fear" from the Latin "veritus," or "mankind" from the Latin "vir."[20] Since Vere is not an allegorical character, Withim's suggested ambiguities have a certain plausibility to them. Hawthorne's metaphors of the heart and head which represent, respectively, human love and compassion as against the human intellect out of touch with the "magnetic chain of humanity" may also symbolize the characters of Billy Budd and Claggart. Again, Vere would be a synthesis of heart and head. One could view the *Indomitable* as an Eden in microcosm on which the fall of man is enacted, or as William Braswell

[20] Phil Withim, "*Billy Budd:* The Testament of Resistance," *Modern Language Quarterly,* XX (June, 1959), p. 125.

suggests, the *Indomitable* may represent Christendom in a death struggle with the powers of atheism set in motion by the French Revolution.[21]

Ray B. West, Jr., argues that the ship, the *Rights of Man*, is a symbol of the Hobbesian outlook in which the state of nature predominates. While on the *Rights of Man* Billy enjoys true freedom. In this somewhat anarchic state he is able to be his natural uncorrupted self. Aboard the *Indomitable*, however, he must live under the law and discipline that one associates with the Lockean outlook, but he is too unsophisticated to do so to his profit.[22] In this sense he is unequal to the Dansker, the old sea Chiron who is able to survive because of his intuitive grasp of the realities of evil and the ways of men. In short, Billy, like Huck Finn and perhaps Holden Caulfield, is better suited to the life of the noble savage. The artificialities of civilization pose problems for him with which he cannot cope.

The symbolic interpretations presented thus far are for the most part conventional, simplistic, and rather obvious. But, to the young student who has had little experience in analyzing literature these interpretations may prove nothing short of revelatory. After the student has learned to interpret symbols at the level suggested in this discussion, the teacher may then introduce him to some of the more esoteric interpretations of professional critics, interpretations whose validity is often open to serious question. Expanding upon the comments made earlier by Saul Bellow, Hans Guth observes unmistakable elements in modern criticism:

Encouraged by the example of critics like Kenneth Burke and William Empson in an uncontrolled free-association technique, teachers made part symbolic of a whole, quality symbolic of object, and object symbolic of anything associated with it in time, place, shape of previous literature, until every object in literary work could mean everything except itself. Followers of an oversimplified Freudianism saw in every girl a Jocasta, in every straight object a phallic symbol. Jungians, unsatisfied with the poignant emotional impact of a representative human situation, felt impelled to go beyond it to the discovery of a mythical archetype of obscure human relevance.[23]

[2] Ray B. West, Jr., "The Unity of *Billy Budd*," *Hudson Review*, V. (Spring, 1925), pp. 120–27.

[3] Hans P. Guth, *English Today and Tomorrow* (Englewood Cliffs: Prentice-Hall, 1964), p. 20.

[4] William Braswell, "Melville's *Billy Budd* as an inside Narrative," *American Literature*, XXIX (May, 1957), p. 133.

One sees this kind of critical attitude in Bernard S. Oldsey's symbolic interpretation of the name of Holden Caulfield. Oldsey interprets Holden to mean William Holden, and Caulfield to mean Joan
Caulfield. Both of these persons were leading Hollywood personalities
of the late 1940's, and their symbolic association with Holden is supposed to represent his neurotic attachment to the movies.[24] Certainly,
Hollywood looms important in Holden's life as a symbol of sham and
phoniness, and he makes many explicit statements that indicate this
attitude. It hardly seems necessary, however, that this attitude needs
further illumination through symbolic references to leading Hollywood
celebrities in the manner suggested by Oldsey; that is, had Holden's
name been anything other than what it is, the reader would hardly be
deprived of important symbols relating to and clarifying theme. Oldsey
does likewise with regard to Sally Hayes' fixation of keeping her kings
in the back row of the checkerboard. Obviously, this idiosyncrasy indicates a certain insecurity and defensiveness in her nature. But Oldsey
suggests that her action relates to the book *King's Row*, in which incest
is an important motif, on the grounds that Sally's stepfather is sexually
attracted to her.[25] However, in all fairness to Oldsey, he does admit
that the "king's row" symbol may be ambiguous and elusive.[26] Yet one
questions whether, for the most part, this kind of interpretation is overdone and far-fetched.

Some of R. W. Stallman's interpretations of the symbolism of *The
Red Badge of Courage* have been seriously questioned by many critics.
A case in point: Stallman states that "Crane's image is used at a crucial
point in the narrative and with symbolic import (as I see it), the wafer
of the sun representing the wafer of the mass."[27] As Oldsey interprets
the significance of Holden's initials, so, too, does Stallman interpret the
initials of Jim Conklin to stand for Jesus Christ, and his action in wash-
ing his shirt before the battle as a rite symbolizing the way to achieve
spiritual salvation.[28] Richard Chase (who has a tendency to be somewhat ingenious as a symbol interpreter himself) takes issue with Stall-

[24] Bernard S. Oldsey, "The Movies in the Rye," *College English*, XXIII (December,
1961). p. 210.
[25] *Ibid.*, p. 213.
[26] *Ibid.*, p. 214.
[27] R. W. Stallman, "Kipling's Wafer and Crane's," in Bradley, *Red Badge*, pp. 167–68.
[28] R. W. Stallman, "Notes Toward an Analysis of *Red Badge*," in Bradley, *Red Badge*,
p. 253.

man's method of interpretation. He cannot accept, for example, Stall-man's equating "sun" with "son" as a pun which is supposed to suggest a God-the-Father, God-the-Son relationship. He does not see Crane as

a symbolist of the sort Mr. Stallman makes him out to be. If he is a symbolist at all, it is only in the sense that any writer with a poetic turn of mind will inevitably introduce symbols into his writing. But the symbols are local and limited in reference, and sometimes they seem no more than decorative.[29]

Phillip Rahv labels Stallman's insight as "the fallacy of misplaced concreteness."[30] Rahv views the wafer as nothing more nor less than an effective Imagist symbol,[31] and criticizes Stallman for reading so much religious significance into the symbols of simple sense experience.[32] Rahv and Chase, it seems, would apply to Crane's imagist prose Archibald MacLeish's proposition in his poem "Ars Poetica" that poetic language must "be" not "mean" if it is to achieve its optimum effect as art. This is, of course, an extreme Imagist position which can be as extremely denotative as Stallman's position is connotative.

Although Chase takes the conventional Imagist position with regard to Crane, he does not do so with regard to Melville. In fact, he interprets some of the symbolism of *Billy Budd* in substantially the same manner that he criticizes Stallman for in his interpretation of the symbolism in *The Red Badge of Courage*. One cannot argue too strenuously with his basic premise that "The real theme of *Billy Budd* is castration and cannibalism, the ritual murder and eating of the host"[33] and that Billy's stutter represent a fear of castration.[34] These interpretations, though not absolutely indisputable, are at least consistent with the basic tenets of Sigmund Freud and Sir James Frazer whose theories of human behavior enjoy some validity among many serious critics. But when he applies his premise to chapter twenty-seven, one of the digressions in *Billy Budd*, his argument seems at best fanciful, and at worst incredible. In this very short chapter of approximately four hundred words, the ship's surgeon and the purser, standing over Billy's body

[29] Richard Chase, ed., "Introduction" to Crane's *The Red Badge of Courage*, p. ix.

[30] Rahv, "The Symbolic Fallacy in Crane Criticism," in Bradley, *Red Badge*, p. 291.

[31] *Ibid.*, p. 292.

[32] *Ibid.*, p. 293.

[33] Richard Chase, *Herman Melville: A Critical Study* (New York: Macmillan, 1949), p. 269.

[34] *Ibid.*, p. 273.

which is lying on a pallet, are engaged in a conversation concerning the peculiar lack of muscular spasm in the body. The dialogue is comical in spots. The surgeon, a dogmatic empiricist, sees no significance in the fact that there is no muscular spasm of any kind. He dismisses the effects of will power or euthanasia as metaphysical fantasy. The purser, however, attributes the lack to some mystical forces beyond the realm of scientific explanation. Richard Chase concludes that, "The sexual spasm does not occur in Billy Budd because Billy's vitality or virtue has been symbolically transferred to Vere."[35] This seems a very far-fetched conclusion because there is nothing in the text that even remotely suggests a sexual spasm, and such a spasm is not normally to be expected from a corpse, although other muscles may be spastic.[36]

The young student is often inclined to indulge in the kinds of interpretation arrived at by critics like Oldsey, Stallman, and Chase; but it is the teacher's job to help the student to avoid this kind of pitfall. Yet the student, who ought to be made aware of these more fanciful interpretations for the sake of his education, might justly argue that if professional critics are free to indulge in such speculation, then why may not he. First, the teacher could point out that all criticism to some degree is fanciful and artificial because the most accurate statement made about a work is the work itself. The criticism at best only serves to make the statement more comprehensible to the reader. Secondly, students do not have the skill or the sophistication that a professional critic has in developing a controversial interpretation. Thus, questionable criticism well written is always better than questionable criticism poorly written. And thirdly, despite the fact that Chase, Stallman, and Fiedler may at times be "way out" in their interpretations, the vast majority of the time they are not, and at best their observations and insights are often of immense value to less gifted readers in aiding and promoting appreciation. Even so, the teacher must permit the student to indulge in some free-wheeling interpretations if for no other reason than to have a means to get the student to reread the work being considered, and it is to be hoped, to reexamine his original interpretation. One may disagree with Chase's premise in regard to the surgeon-purser dialogue, but Chase's statement does encourage the reader to peruse Melville's text carefully, and to become more involved in the critical process. Thus

[35] *Ibid.*, p. 275.
[36] Pathologists will verify this point.

does Chase's esoteric premise serve a useful function. One might even hope that Chase himself could have been moved to reexamine his assumptions.

As was suggested earlier, colors may be used to symbolize many nuances of human experience. Perhaps there is no passage in American literature in which this is done more effectively than in "The Whiteness of the Whale," a chapter in *Moby Dick*. Here Melville catalogues in vivid detail the various experiences that whiteness connotes: terror, mystery, joy, innocence, purity, and many others. In a grim passage in *The Adventures of Huckleberry Finn*, Mark Twain depicts Pap Finn as he really is in a paragraph in which whiteness predominates as a sort of "subjective correlative": "There warn't no color in his face, where his face showed; it was white; not like another man's white, but a white to make a body sick, a white to make a body's flesh crawl, a tree toad white, a fish-belly white."[37]

The concept of whiteness is given substance in the form of snow as a major image in several of the works of this discussion. In Conrad Aiken's "Silent Snow, Secret Snow" the image predominates. The young lad whose mind is deteriorating in a Kafkaesque manner is obsessed with visions of snow. It becomes "a wall behind which he could retreat into heavenly seclusion."[38] "Its beauty was paralyzing— beyond all words, all experience, all dream."[39] The image is completed at the same time that the lad becomes fully schizophrenic: "The hiss was now becoming a roar—the whole world was a vast moving screen of snow—but even now it said peace, it said remoteness, is said cold, it said sleep."[40] In Cather's "Paul's Case" snow serves to soothe Paul as he looks out from his hotel window. In effect it desensitizes him to the world about him and prepares him for his suicidal leap. The snow symbolizes the nihilistic state he so desires. Snow is an important image in Capote's *Other Voices, Other Rooms* since it symbolizes the freedom that the young Negro girl Zoo seeks in the North. She never sees the snow, however, for she is brutally raped and reduced to idiocy before she can leave the South.

[37] Samuel Langhorne Clemens, *The Adventures of Huckleberry Finn* (New York: New American Library, 1964), p. 27.
[38] Conrad Aiken, "Silent Snow, Secret Snow," in Thurston, p. 349.
[39] *Ibid.*, p. 357.
[40] *Ibid.*, p. 364.

Prep schools figure as prominent symbols in three of the works treated in this discussion. To Holden Caulfield, Pency Prep symbolizes the phoniness about which he is so distressed and preoccupied; to Amory Blaine, St. Regis symbolizes social advancement and preferment; to Gene Forrester, Devon symbolizes the crucible in which he is matured through a painful process of purification.

The symbolism in *The Bear* is discernible at a basic level. In a sense the bear, like Moby Dick, is an impersonal force of nature, both respected and feared by men. As Moby Dick is scarred by harpoons, so is the bear scarred by bullets and traps. As a symbol the bear is probably somewhat easier to interpret than is Moby Dick. One can even discern allegorical elements in him. He represents both the Indian and the Negro whom the white man has exploited. In a more specific sense he represents Sam Fathers, whose death occurs, significantly, at the same time as the bear's. The tainted land which Ike refuses as his inheritance symbolizes the transmitted guilt of his progenitors, and Ike's self-imposed exile as a carpenter in the wilderness suggests a Christ motif.

In *Winesburg, Ohio* Anderson employs the effective symbol of the human grotesque: "The moment one of the people took one of the truths to himself, called it his truth, and tried to live his life by it, he became a grotesque and the truth he embraced became a falsehood."[41] It is interesting to note that George Willard does not become a grotesque. He learns to manage experience so as not to allow it to distort his vision of reality. But this is not the case with many others, such as Dr. Reefy, the lonely widower, whose frustrations are symbolized by the bits of paper which he rolls up into little gnarled balls after recording his most intimate thoughts on them.

One could list many other meaningful symbols which appear in the works considered here. Lucas Beauchamp's golden toothpick in *Intruder in the Dust* symbolizes his unquenchable pride and his utter defiance of the white man, as well as a status symbol in the Negro community. The Dixieland, the boarding house in *Look Homeward, Angel*, symbolizes Eugene's shame for his mother's crass materialism, and the nicotine-yellowed fingers of his brother Steve symbolize dissipation and degeneracy. The graceful gestures and nimble fingers of Wings Biddle-baum in *Winesburg, Ohio* symbolize the futility of his efforts as a young man to realize his natural talents. The Morses in *Martin Eden* symbolize

[41] Anderson, p. 25.

the debilitated bourgeois whom Martin eventually comes to despise. The tree in *A Separate Peace* symbolizes the ritual device from which the boys jump in preparation for war. The mountains in *The Red Pony* symbolize the mysteries of death for young Jody.

Man is the symbol-making animal par excellence, and his symbol-making facility is most often expressed through his system of spoken and written language. Because man deals so frequently with symbols, he often tends to confuse them with the realities for which they stand, and thus do symbols often become ends in themselves rather than means to ends. The purpose of literary study is to provide pleasure and understanding for the reader, and through symbols this end may be more effectively realized. The statements of Stone, Bellow, and Guth quoted in this chapter indicate that the interpretation of symbols can take two extremes: one in which the symbol and its referent are equated absolutely by a process of transubstantiation; the other in which the symbol and its referent becomes loosely independent of each other by a process of consubstantiation. In the former, essence is emphasized; in the latter, accident. Ideally, a balance should be struck between these two extremes.

4

Irony and paradox as style

Like symbolism, irony and paradox depend upon connotation to assist in the illumination and development of content. Ordinarily, however, the language of irony and paradox does not depend on metaphor, simile, or personification to achieve its effects. Instead, it is often highly denotative and literal at times, and its effects can easily be missed by the careless reader. In order to discern irony and paradox and to appreciate these devices of style to their fullest extent, the reader is often obliged to devote extraordinary care to his reading of the text. Otherwise he may miss the many subtleties that the author has taken great pains to enmesh in the work.

Actually, irony and paradox are for all practical purposes synonomous terms; that is, every irony can be expressed in terms of paradox, and every paradox in terms of irony, often with but slight rewording, and with no significant distortion of meaning. Yet the two terms are not absolutely synonomous. A teacher can often be hard pressed to explain to the student the exact difference between them. Laurence Perrine defines the terms with a clarity and precision that meet the needs of the high school teacher and the common reader, when he states that paradox is "an apparent contradiction which is nevertheless somehow true."[1] One could observe many phenomena in human experience which are paradoxical: through sorrow often comes joy; loss can lead to gain; in ugliness there may be beauty; and death, symbolic or real, can produce life.

An excellent composition technique that the teacher may employ to draw out the student's native awareness of the nature of paradox is to present him with the topic sentence: "Although war is intrinsically evil, it yet creates much good." One might limit this to the war situation

[1] Perrine, *Sound and Sense*, p. 90.

in *The Red Badge of Courage* or in *Billy Budd*, or apply it to war in general. In any case, the perceptive student will see that on the positive side war promotes national unity and solidarity, encourages scientific research, provides jobs, liberates subjugated peoples, and nurtures humanitarianism in ways often impossible to achieve in peace time. The student can develop his composition with these and other arguments in mind. Of course, as must be pointed out, it is always morally preferable in real-life situations to bring about good ends without recourse to evil. But, then, this would not be paradoxical because there is no apparent contradiction involved.

Perrine discusses three kinds of irony: verbal, dramatic, and situational. In verbal irony, in which understatement is often employed, one thing is said but another thing is meant; in dramatic irony there is a discrepancy between what a fictional character says, what the author really means, or what reality indicates. Dramatic irony is often called unconscious irony because the character is unaware of the discrepancy. In situational irony one's anticipation of an action or an outcome is at odds with its realization.[2] The three types of irony have in common the element of the unexpected, the opposite of what one usually anticipates in human affairs. Thus, in the workings of irony and paradox there is an element of reverse logic, a subtle discrepancy between cause and effect, between appearance and reality.

It is essential that the student develop a sensitivity to the workings of irony and paradox if he is to become a perceptive, intelligent reader, for the ability to discern the nuances of irony and paradox gives one a special insight into truth. In all irony and paradox there is a constant dialectic between appearances and realities taking place, between what seems and what is. The literal language of irony and paradox presents appearances; the figurative overtones of the literal language present realities. Thus is the style of irony and paradox akin to the style of symbolism in that one thing (appearances) stands for and clarifies another (realities).

The ability to distinguish between appearance and reality requires an intellectual effort on the part of the reader, and as one reads more and enlarges his apperceptive mass of experiences this effort becomes less burdensome and more rewarding. Cleanth Brooks, a leading exponent of the belief that irony and paradox are of the essence in the figurative

[2] *Ibid.*, pp. 93–97.

expressions of superior art as against the literal statements of science remarks: "It is the scientist whose truth requires a language purged of every trace of paradox."[3] For "The tendency of science is necessarily to stabilize terms, to freeze them into strict denotations; the poet's tendency is by contrast disruptive. The terms are continually modifying each other, and thus violating their dictionary meanings."[4] Thus do irony and paradox serve to expand and clarify content through the interplay of connotations in counterpoint with denotations.

In all good art, content is presented and developed indirectly in order to allow the reader to earn through his own intellectual efforts the experience that the art work is trying to convey. An earned experience is always more meaningful than a fully presented one because one has earned it through his own efforts, with little outside help. The artist in his creative act provides the reader with a partially complete work to which he must apply himself if he is to participate fully in the experience of the work. In this sense the reader becomes a co-creator of sorts with the artist. It is also the author's responsibility to provide the reader with workable clues so that the reader may reconstruct the content of the work sensibly. Often the inexperienced reader is unable to detect the artist's clues, and thus he grossly misreads the work. Most especially are irony and paradox misread. One can observe this most revealingly (and even humorously) when the young student attempts his first reading of a work like Swift's "A Modest Proposal." All this argues a case for correct guidance on the part of the teacher so that the student will not become victim to the kind of occurence that Wayne Booth relates:

An intelligent friend of mine has admitted to using the works of Huxley throughout his adolescence as a steady source of pornography. The orgies satirized in *Brave New World* were for him genuinely orgiastic, with no comic or satiric crosslights. . . . Most of us, especially if we have read widely when young without guidance from more experienced readers, can recall misreadings of this kind.[5]

The student must see that paradox works by virtue of its shock value, and that "by the fact of its apparent absurdity, it underscores

[3] Cleanth Brooks, *The Well-Wrought Urn* (New York: Harcourt, Brace & World, 1947), p. 3.

[4] *Ibid.*, p. 8.

[5] Wayne C. Booth, *The Rhetoric of Fiction* (Chicago: The University of Chicago Press, 1965), p. 389.

the truth of what is being said." So, too, does irony achieve its fullest impact indirectly, often by understatement as against overstatement. The artist who can handle irony and paradox skillfully is, so to speak, driving a spike into oak with a tack hammer; but when an artist has to resort to overstatement to emphasize a truth in preference to the effective understatement that characterizes so much well-constructed irony, he is, in effect, driving a tack into balsa with a sledge hammer. This is not to say, however, that overstatement or hyperbole does not have merit as a rhetorical device. It is to say, however, that, ordinarily, overstatement is out of place in irony. Nor is it intended that the analogy of the tack hammer and the spike need only apply to effective irony. It applies indeed to all well-conceived rhetoric in which language is employed to achieve optimum effect.[6]

The problem of appearance versus reality occurs in many forms in *The Adventures of Huckleberry Finn*, and thus irony permeates almost every incident and situation in the work. There is high irony in the fact that Pap Finn reviles Huck for going to school and acquiring dandified ways. Ordinarily, one expects responsible fathers to encourage their children to become educated and cultivated. Students are often humorously amazed at Pap Finn's behavior in this regard. His comments to Huck aptly illustrate verbal and dramatic irony. There is further irony in Pap Finn's resolution, which he makes to Judge Thatcher, to mend his ways and to live a virtuous life. For within twenty-four hours after having made it, Pap tumbles into his old ways again. When Pap "cusses" the law for stealing Huck from him after all the sacrifices he has made as a parent, for denying him Huck's $6,000 fortune, and for allowing Negroes to have rights at the expense of the white man, he is indulging in unconscious irony of the highest order. His words indicate one thing, but reality, with which he is completely out of touch, indicates another.

There is irony in many of the situations in which Huck is involved. He takes delight in watching the search for his "drowned" body. His inducing the watchman at the wharf to free the stranded criminals and his employing reverse psychology to ward off the bounty hunters bring to light some ugly truths in regard to human greed, cupidity, and disingenuousness. Huck's involvement with the Shepherdsons and the Grangerfords provides him with many insights into the workings of irony. Buck's explanation of the origin and nature of feuds is an object

---

[6] Perrine, *Sound and Sense*, p. 91.

lesson on how the evil of senseless killing can be made to appear honorable, and how Satanic human pride can be made to appear as the most lofty human idealism. The crowning irony of the Shepherdson-Grangerford feud occurs on the Sunday that the families attend church together. After the services they amicably discuss the "uplift" values of a good sermon. They are even so noble as to leave their guns outside the church while divine services are in progress. Later in the day, however, when they learn that Harney Shepherdson and Sophia Grangerford have eloped a dreadful carnage ensues. The irony springs from the fact that the marriage of the two lovers should have resolved the families' differences, but instead it only intensifies their mutual hatreds. Harney and Sophia escape, but the remaining members of the two families virtually wipe one another out. This is a reversal of what happens in Shakespeare's *Romeo and Juliet*, in which the two lovers die and effect a reconciliation of their families. There is a paradox in the fact that Harney and Sophia have to bring about the death of their entire families in order to make it possible to give life to a new generation in which the two family strains are combined. Thus is reconciliation achieved through unfortunate but inevitable destruction. Hatred begets love.

The Duke-Dauphin incidents provide some of the most effective ironies in the work. Both of these scoundrels exploit the townsfolk's incapacity to distinguish appearances from realities, and they are thus able to perpetrate almost unbelievable fraud and deception. Even the young, innocent Wilks girls, who are not blinded by a passion for personal gain, fall their victims. As Huck deceives the wharf watchman through reverse psychology, so, too, does the Dauphin deceive the Wilks girls by "generously" giving them a bag of money which he really expects them to refuse, and indeed it is refused. Later, however, the Duke and the Dauphin are deceived themselves when Huck puts the money in Peter Wilks' coffin and leads them to believe that the money was stolen by the Negro family which they had divided and sold off. The Duke ironically misinterprets the family's intense grief to be playacting, the very device that he and the Dauphin employ in their fraudulent activities. The irony is heightened by the fact that Dr. Robinson and Levi Bell, the town lawyer, who see the Duke and the Dauphin for what they really are, are scorned and maligned by the townsfolk for trying to expose them, and all this despite the overwhelming evidence of their fraudulence. Through the device of irony Mark Twain in these scenes makes a powerful comment on the utter depravity of the common man.

Had he employed a more direct method, lacking in irony, his comment would hardly have had such force. One thinks in this regard of his short story, "The Man Who Corrupted Hadleyburg," in which he vehemently curses the "damned human race." In *The Adventures of Huckleberry Finn* he demonstrates and dramatizes his vision through irony, while in his short story he presents his vision directly in a ranting, raving manner which is aesthetically inferior to his style in *The Adventures of Huckleberry Finn*. The tack-hammer, sledge-hammer analogy could apply here in judging the relative merits of these two works.

Huck Finn himself is far better able to distinguish between appearance and reality than are the Duke and the Dauphin. Because of his ability to discern truth. he is not the victim of ironic reversals, as many of the other characters are. Because he does not intend to deceive maliciously, there is little need for justice to provide a moral corrective for his actions through irony. Despite his sensitivity to the workings of irony, however, he often does not know the full truth of things. He does-not know, for example, that Pap was the dead man on the house raft, or that Jim has always been free. The latter fact serves to reduce his noble efforts to free Jim to naught, and both of these facts create some aesthetic problems in the work which will be treated in the chapter on structure.

Perhaps the one situation in which irony plays the most important part in Huck's experiences occurs when he utters, "All right, then. I'll go to Hell," after he learns that his conscience takes priority over his prejudices. This is unconscious irony because he is not fully aware of the fact that his decision is sanctioned by absolute morality, not community mores. It is one of the few situations in the work in which the reader can see a truth more clearly than Huck can. Elsewhere, the reader and Huck share the same ability to distinguish appearance from reality.

All that has been said thus far with respect to irony can with some rewording apply equally to paradox. The teacher might frame his language in the following manner to illustrate the difference: It is ironic that Huck should fulfill his life through death, but that life should result from death is a paradox. It is ironic that Huck should have religious principles without having a religion, but that religious principles should result from an irreligious or nonreligious attitude is a paradox. In short, irony usually involves the reversal that results with respect to a particular person in a particular situation; paradox, on the other hand, involves the apparent contradictions which result when two antithetical ideas abstracted from a human situation clash but are eventually reconciled.

Billy Budd is a study in the paradoxical nature of good and evil. Mumford points out that

Good and evil exist in the nature of things, each forever itself, each doomed to war with the other. In the working out of human institutions, evil has a place as well as the good: Vere is contemptuous of Claggart, but cannot do without him; he loves Budd as a son and must condemn him to the noose: justice dictates an act abhorrent to his nature. . . . These are the fundamental ambiguities of life.[7]

By nature good and evil are mutually antithetical entities. They are polar opposites. Nevertheless, it is curious that in human situations the two are somehow reconciled and compromised. One is hard pressed to find in human experience any person or thing which typifies pure good or pure evil. Drama or fiction which attempts to do so usually becomes inferior art which relies heavily on melodrama and stock characters to achieve its effects. In fact, only as abstractions can these concepts be grasped by the imagination in pure form.

It is a commonplace paradox that the wicked succeed and the virtuous often fail disastrously. Billy Budd with all his native virtue and innocence is unequal to the wiles of Claggart, or to any problematic situation which requires sophistication to solve, and Billy can never acquire sophistication, for usually only those who have had some involvement with evil can. Often it is the greatest sinners who undergo an intense conversion and become the greatest saints, and in the greatest saints often lies an unexpected potentiality for evil. But Billy, though he has flaws of character, never consciously commits a vicious act, and Claggart, though he has many strengths of character, never consciously effects a positive good. Yet Claggart's evil does lead to some good in that it provides a scapegoat whose immolation promotes the common good by serving to strengthen military and naval discipline. The securing of the common good is accomplished, however, through permitting the evil of taking an innocent life.

[7] Lewis Mumford, *Herman Melville* (New York: Harcourt, Brace & World, 1957), p. 357.

The irony of this situation becomes involved. It is ironic that the wicked should have the power to destroy the virtuous. In Billy's case the irony backfires because Claggart's attempt to destroy him leads to his own destruction. Of course, Claggart's hatred of Billy is so intense that he would willingly suffer his own destruction to ensure Billy's, in the same manner that Iago in *Othello* would endure the pains of hell in exchange for the assurance that Othello would suffer equally. The irony backfires again when Billy's execution, which was to prevent mutiny, almost leads to one; but the mutiny is forestalled, ironically, by the "timely" appearance of the French warship *The Atheiste*, formerly (and ironically) named *The St. Louis*. The irony reaches full circle when the men deify Billy and hold in reverence shavings of the mast from which he has hanged, much as the early Christians venerated pieces of Christ's cross.

One sees in these occurrences a seesaw action in which good and evil do battle but neither is victorious nor defeated, and knowledge of the final outcome seems not to be accessible to human understanding. Raymond M. Weaver resolves this question in his own mind through his paradoxical suggestion: "The powers of evil and horror must be granted their fullest scope; it is only thus we can triumph over them."[8]

Though one must grant that Claggart is an evil person, there is something uncomfortably admirable in his nature. In *Redburn*, Melville suggests this paradoxical kind of admiration in his comment on Milton's Satan:

Though Milton's Satan dilutes our abhorrence with admiration, it is only because he is not a genuine being, but something altered from a genuine original. We gather not from the four gospels alone, any high-raised fancies concerning this Satan; we only know him from thence as the personification of the essence of evil, which, who but pickpockets and burglars will admire? But this takes not from the merit of our high-priest of poetry; it only enhances it, that with such unmitigated evil for his material, he should build up his most goodly structure.[9]

The paradox is further complicated by the fact that though there is cogent evidence that Claggart bears false witness against Billy deliberately and intentionally, Melville in keeping with the Calvinistic ethic

[8] Raymond M. Weaver, *The Shorter Novels of Herman Melville* (New York: Liveright Publishing Corp., 1928), p. ii.
[9] Melville, *Redburn*, p. 265.

yet suggests that perhaps Claggart is not wholly responsible for his actions: "Now something such as one was Claggart, in whom was the mania of an evil nature, not engendered by vicious training or corrupting books or licentious living, but born with him and innate; in short 'a depravity according to nature.' "10

All of Vere's actions are conditioned by irony. His elaborate plan to avoid injustice miscarries and actually causes injustice. When he "wisely" decides to place Billy and Claggart face to face so as to expose Claggart's obvious villainy, he actually worsens the situation by making it possible for Billy to strike Claggart. His having Billy hanged so as to set an example for the crew actually puts the crew in a mutinous state. In short, all his carefully thought-out decisions turn out to be ironic blunders. In devoting much of his introduction to a discussion of the colorful career of the ostentatious and prideful Lord Nelson who, unlike Vere, is less a thinker and more a doer, Melville seems to suggest that the two men are in ironic contrast to each other, that Nelson would have avoided Vere's dilemma by not allowing himself to become ensnared in thought as Vere had done, and by not allowing himself to become personally and emotionally involved with Billy.

The proper interpretation of *Billy Budd* seems crucially to depend upon whether Melville himself is being ironic in his presentation. This is an important question over which critics are divided, but one has to arrive at some sort of an answer in order to determine whether Melville himself viewed Vere as an unfortunate victim of circumstances over which he has little or no control, or as a despicable immoral man, outrageously insensitive to the demands of justice and truth. The views of two representative critics will be discussed here in summary fashion. E. L. Grant Watson argues for the former alternative. He sees Vere's action as a sort of acceptance of, or resignation to, the will of God, and trusts that the wrong will be redressed at a final judgment, "The Last Assizes." Vere takes full responsibility for his action, but though he knows that it is intrinsically wrong, he rationalizes it by arguing that it serves a higher good by being the lesser of two evils. Vere admits by his action that evil is necessary and inevitable in human affairs, and cannot be avoided even by those with the best of intentions.11 In an

10 Melville, *Billy Budd*, p. 738.

11 E. L. Grant Watson, "Melville's Testament of Acceptance," *New England Quarterly*, VI (June, 1933), pp. 319–27.

involved rebuttal Phil Withim argues the latter alternative. Withim cannot accept the argument that Vere acts out of an interest for the common good. Rather, he is cowardly and brutal, and is influenced in his judgment by fear, not reason. Withim would maintain that when Vere upon witnessing Claggart's death utters, "Struck dead by the Angel of God! Yet the Angel must hang,"[12] he is revealing prejudgment of Billy and bowing to an evil necessity. Thus Vere's later "reasonings" are in reality clever rationalizations. Withim get himself into a difficult position with this interpretation because he refuses to read the phrase "virtuous necessity" as a paradox. Rather, he reads it literally, and thus takes it to be outright contradiction rather than paradox. He is in effect demanding an absolute morality.[13] Most students find it difficult to brand Vere as a scoundrel and a coward. Withim's literal position in effect rules out the possibility of Vere's being a true tragic victim, or of Melville's having any true sympathy for him. The Vere problem will be referred to again in the chapter on tragedy.

If Melville had intended for the reader to interpret Vere as a coward and a scoundrel, he would have made his comments on Vere more obviously ironic, as he does in the conclusion of the work through the device of a newspaper article. The irony in this account is so obvious that only the most obtuse student could possible miss it, and so devastating in its rhetorical effects as to merit expanded quotation:

John Claggart ... discovering that some sort of plot was incipient among an inferior section of the ship's company, and that the ring leader was one William Budd . . . in the act of arraigning the man before the Captain was vindictively stabbed to the heart. . . . The enormity of the crime and the extreme depravity of the criminal appear the greater in view of the character of the victim, a middle-aged man respectable and discreet.[14]

The predominant paradox of *The Red Badge of Courage* is that cowardice begets courage. This statement is also the theme of Henry Fleming's experiential development, and it is symbolized most dramatically by means of his accidental wound. Contributing to the total effect of the paradox is the sum total of all the verbal, situational and dramatic ironies in the work. Thus do symbolism, irony, and paradox

---

[12] Melville, *Billy Budd*, p. 749.

[13] Withim, pp. 115–27.

[14] Melville, *Billy Budd*, pp. 761–62.

as elements of style give substance to character and theme, the elements of content. Enough has been said of the action in *The Red Badge of Courage* in this discussion thus far to cover adequately the main ironies of the work. However, there is one situation that deserves special consideration, for it may well contain the most important single irony in the work.

When Henry in his fear takes flight like the proverbial chicken, he is unnoticed by his fellow soldiers. This is because on the battle ground, unlike the parade ground, an army is in disarray. In the confusion of the moment it is hard to tell who is running and who is charging. The confusion is compounded by the fact that the smoke and the dust make it harder to see, and that a soldier's concern for himself and his fear of the enemy dampens his awareness of what his fellow soldier is doing. All this proves to be Henry's salvation. It would be impossible to initiate court-martial proceedings against him for cowardice for there are no witnesses to testify against him, and his flesh wound appears to be proof that he stood his ground. Henry, of course, is not conscious of this as he makes his way back to the regiment, and he is exhilarated to learn after his hero's welcome that only he is aware of the truth. Yet the fact remains that from the standpoint of the letter of the law he is guilty of cowardice. And, as a result of this discrepancy between appearance and reality, Henry gets a second chance. The irony of these circumstances gains even greater significance when one compares Henry's situation with Billy Budd's. Both boys react instinctively and spontaneously in an act of self-preservation. One is court-martialed and hanged, and the other is eventually given a hero's acclaim. Their situations differ mainly in that one situation is witnessed, and the other is not. All this goes to suggest that in the workings of irony there is often a certain fatalism in which there is little justice and logic. It argues a case for the importance of chance and determinism as against free will as crucial elements in the ordering of human affairs. The student would do well to read at this point the chapter "The Mat Maker" in *Moby Dick* in which Melville through the imagery of the woof and the warp in the texture of a woven mat considers the mysterious interrelationships which exist between chance, necessity (fate), and will.

In *The Catcher in the Rye* Holden Caulfield becomes the victim of an entire complex of ironies. Essentially, Holden sets out to correct the contradictions and tensions that irony and paradox bring to his experience. A natural Platonist, Holden is in quest of pure reality, untainted by the accidents of appearance. Often he confronts reality directly, but he is unable to cope with it, unable to adapt to its demands, and thus unable to order his experience sensibly.

His ability to distinguish appearance from reality is often remarkable, but not consistent. He perceives immediately human dishonesty, insincerity, selfishness, pretense, and callousness. In fact, one might even say that he overperceives these qualities in others, and often makes more out of them than justice and charity allow. His repeated use of the word "phony" and his constant "If you want to know the truth" serve as linguistic devices which signal his perceptions. And, in his first-person narrative presentation, he is in effect sharing with the reader his perceptions of realities by stripping these realities of the appearances which obscure them.

But, not only does Holden interpret reality as he sees it, he also reveals his true self to the reader in the process. It is an outstanding irony of the work that the very words he employs to strip realities from appearances reveal characteristics of himself of which he is scarcely aware. Thus do his statements often become masterpieces of unconscious irony, and how truly does he prove that when Peter speaks of Paul we learn more of Peter than of Paul. In this regard he differs substantially from Huck Finn, who is, for the most part, on parity with the reader in that the reader and he share practically the same knowledge of him (Huck).

At his worst, Holden displays the same faults for which he so bitterly criticizes others. He criticizes Ackley for his vulgar, annoying habits, yet through his silly playacting and his impertinent questions he purposely provokes in Ackley the same disgust and discomfort that Ackley provokes in him. He brands Stradlater as the "secret slob," and passes moral judgment on him for his "giving the time" to the girls. Yet, Jane Gallagher, whom Stradlater probably seduces, is the same girl that Holden tries to seduce earlier, but fails. She does not even permit him to kiss her on the mouth. Furthermore, Holden violates his own puritanical standards of sex in his willingness to engage the services of a call girl. Of course, he rationalizes his behavior by arguing that the experience will provide him with the know-how to become a good husband, a rationalization that he would quickly brand as "phony" in anyone else.

Holden complains that no one ever listens to him, yet he never gives Mr. Spencer or Mr. Antolini a full hearing when one of them speaks. Holden's ironic lack of self-knowledge is revealed most tellingly in his maudlin desire to be the "catcher" who in messianic fashion preserves the purity and innocence of the young, and in his overstated outrage when he sees foul words on public walls. These reactions indicate a mis-application of energy in his effort to correct the discrepancies that exist between appearances and realities. Holden is intensely aware that something is sadly out of joint in the world of humankind, but he is less aware that something is lacking within him, something that has more to do with himself than with others. And, this imbalance of awarenesses causes him to fall into the error of mistaking appearances and realities in a way that Huck Finn could never do. It was suggested earlier that Holden's real failure as a human being lies in his incapacity for true charity. Irony gives substance to this suggestion by further suggesting that it is really his failure to perceive his incapacity for true charity that causes him to fail as a person. In this light his desire to be the "catcher" reduces itself to quixotic gush, though he presents his desire as a noble sentiment.

All this does not mean that Holden is an out-and-out hypocrite, a thoroughly insincere and disingenuous person. It does mean, however, that those who, like Edgar Branch and others, would see Holden as a saint or an unfortunate victim of a cruel and unfeeling adult world are probably not attending carefully to the ironic overtones of Holden's utterances, but, rather, are taking his words too literally. Like Holden, they fail to see in him what he fails to see in himself. Irony serves, then, to reveal the whole truth of the matter, and the truth lies somewhere between the two extremes of interpretation. In his first reading of *The Catcher in the Rye*, the young student usually sympathizes and identifies with Holden passionately. Rarely does he hold him in complete con-tempt. On subsequent rereadings, however, especially if under the guidance of a teacher who has a more than conventional awareness of the ironic nuances of the work, the student usually takes a more moder-ate view of Holden.

The main irony of Faulkner's *The Bear* can be related to Robert Frost's poem "The Gift Outright." The first line of the poem, "The land was ours before we were the land's," aptly sums up the reason for Ike's guilt: the premature ravishing of the virgin land at the expense of the Indian who had a natural claim to it, and of the Negro who was forced to live on it and make it productive for the benefit of the white man, who is unconscious of his transgression. Ike cannot endure the injustice of this double outrage, and thus he is driven to atone for it. Were he not as sensitive to the workings of irony as he is, and as able to distinguish appearance from reality, he would not have been endowed with such a keen sense of guilt and justice. In short, his virtue results from his understanding of irony.

Chick Mallison of *Intruder in the Dust* finds himself in a situation similar to Ike's. Both boys are thoroughly conscious of the immoral effects of injustice, and both set out to do something positive to correct injustice. It is ironic, at least in the eyes of the typical Southerner, that Chick, a white youth of sixteen, his young Negro friend Alec Sander, and a spinster of seventy would "violate the grave of one of its [the community's] progeny in order to save a nigger murderer from its vengeance."[15] It is also ironic that it should fall to the very young and the very old, the most ineffectual members of a society, to correct that society's injustice. The basic paradox in *Intruder in the Dust* is that injustice can be made to appear just, and that through injustice, justice can be more forcefully realized.

Sarty Snopes of "Barn Burning" does not share Ike's and Chick's perceptions of irony, though he does share their sense of justice and integrity. He becomes the victim of unconscious irony after his father's death as he sobs, "Father. My Father. . . . He was brave. . . . He was in the war. He was in Colonel Sartoris' cav'ry."[16] Sarty, of course, knows that his father was a freebooter out for bounty, friend's or foe's. Sarty is unable to see reality in its entirety because his blood ties blur his vision. The reader, however, is completely able to distinguish appearances from realities, and to sympathize with Sarty.

The main irony in *A Separate Peace* lies in the fact that Finney, who at first seems to be a tyrannical, imposing character is in reality almost unbelievably modest, trusting, and childlike. The reader gets the mistaken impression because Finney is being presented from Gene Forrester's point of view. In time Gene realizes what Finney's true nature is and shares this new insight with the reader. Even so, there are many

[15] William Faulkner, *Intruder in the Dust* (New York: Modern Library, 1948,) p. 94.
[16] William Faulkner, "Barn Burning," in Thurston, pp. 238–39.

hints of Finney's true nature which the careful reader can perceive long before Gene becomes aware of it. For example, Finney risks his life to save Gene from falling from the tree. He praises Gene for his intellectual achievements. Later, ironically, Gene deliberately causes Finney to fall from the tree. Finney displays his modesty when, with Gene as the only witness, he breaks the standing record for the crawl stroke in the school pool, a feat he accomplishes without even training for. He refuses to let anyone else know of this accomplishment because he wants to share it only with Gene. In reality it is an act of pure love for Finney to take this attitude, but Gene misinterprets it as a ruse to continue his tyrannic hold over him. The irony reaches macabre proportions when Finney's death is caused by a piece of bone marrow from his injured leg which gets into his blood stream and clogs his heart. Gene's inability to distinguish appearances from realities gives rise to the paradox that love begets hatred.

In *On the Road* a series of paradoxes is evident. The main characters achieve a personal stability of sorts through living disordered, disoriented lives; they find reason in the irrational, and morality in the immoral. As they approach unconsciousness by becoming totally immersed in their various unconventional experiences, their conscious perceptions seem to increase, and they attain to their version of the beatific vision. This is most tellingly revealed in Sal Paradise's paradoxical comment on Dean Moriarty: "I suddenly realized that Dean, by virtue of his enormous series of sins, was becoming the Idiot, the Imbecile, the Saint of the lot. . . . The Holy Goof."[17] Thus are flux and chaos transformed into tranquility and serenity through the medium of paradox. The characters in this work are in ironic contrast to Holden Caulfield, who is unable to create order out of the chaos that is his life. Indeed, to these characters the very stability that Holden yearns for would prove unendurable.

Unable to resolve the inner tensions that result when appearance and reality clash, Martin Eden resorts to suicide. He cannot bear to be deceived by appearances, nor can he adapt to the demands of reality. He thus finds himself in a frightful quandary. In this respect he is like Holden Caulfield, whose mental breakdown can be likened to Martin's suicide. Moreover, Holden does think of suicide several times, and displays the potential to perform the act. He does not do so, however, be-

17 Kerouac, p. 160.

cause he does not experience the total despair that Martin does. Eden differs from Huck Finn, Ike McCaslin, and Henry Fleming in that these heroes, paradoxically, commit a kind of suicide which leads to a more fulfilling life, in their willingness to confront and reorder new experience, and build upon the devitalized experience of the past. In a mystical and religious sense, Billy Budd does likewise.

By nature Martin is a paradoxical person. He is coarse, yet sensitive to beauty; brutal, yet tender; a doer, yet a thinker; a Nietzschean individualist, yet a Marxian socialist. He cannot reconcile these differences into a satisfactory synthesis. Within him the forces of inner, other, and tradition direction grapple with each other. Unlike Ishmael, of *Moby Dick*, who comes to terms with the contradictions of his experience, Martin is unable to grasp the meaning of paradox. This is ironic in itself because Martin has the qualities of mind which are necessary to understand paradox.

Martin's disillusionment begins when he comes to realize that people are not what they appear to be. This discrepancy is most tellingly illustrated through Ruth Morse, whom Martin at first worships and adores. As he becomes more cultured and educated, however, her qualities begin to appear to him tarnished and tainted, and finally he comes to see her as a hollow shell of a woman. Paralleling this development is Martin's ironic realization that he himself is undergoing a drastic change in the sense that his self-education, which is far superior to the formal education of the college graduates in Ruth Morse's circle of friends, gives him insights into ugly truths that in his uneducated state he could scarcely have imagined, truths that he is totally unprepared to cope with. What Martin can least endure is the irony that he is lionized after his success as a writer by those very people who scorned and rejected him before his success. Ruth begs his forgiveness; his despicable brother-in-law Higgenbotham virtually grovels before him; society at large shows a new respect for him. The hypocrisy of this unexpected adulation proves too much for him, and prods him on to self-destruction. Thus do his attempts to fulfill himself become the ironic instruments of his undoing.

The predominant irony in *An American Tragedy* is seen in the fact that Clyde Griffiths is never more ready for reform and rehabilitation than he is at the time that he spends his last days in death row after being condemned to death. While isolated from society he is able to see the foolishness and immorality of his ways, and with the help of Reverend McMillan acquires the state of mind which could well serve as the first step to a remarkable self-reformation. Society is blind to this subtle truth, however, and destroys the very person whom it has a moral obligation to try to save, especially since it is partially responsible for Clyde's predicament. Thus through irony is society doubly indicted both in what it causes and in what it fails to correct. As an object lesson in the possibilities of personal rehabilitation, the student might study the career of Nathan Leopold, who, together with Richard Loeb, committed one of the most terrible murders of the twentieth century, and who is now living a useful, productive life as a teacher in Puerto Rico.

Early in his voyage to England, young Redburn painfully learns of the discrepancies that exist between appearances and realities. He is shocked, for example, when he sees how Captain Riga's behavior changes so markedly at sea. In port he is gracious, charming, affable, and fastidious in his personal habits. At sea he is brutal, domineering, and unkempt. Many of Redburn's romantic illusions are shattered also. He becomes the victim of the meanness and brutality of the hardened sailors aboard ship, and sees the great city of Liverpool for the fleshpot of evil and corruption that it is. In his associations with and his observations of the Satanic Jackson he experiences the paradoxical discomforts of ambivalence. Though he hates Jackson, he yet pities him; though he finds Jackson wicked, he yet sees something mysteriously beautiful in him; though he fears him, he yet respects him and is fascinated by him. Redburn's counterpart, Robin, of "My Kinsman, Major Molineux," is initiated into his first real insight into reality when he sees his uncle for the first time. Up to this moment he had encountered appearances which pointed to some vague, strangely mysterious reality, elusive but pending. Comparatively speaking, reality unfolds for Redburn by degrees. For Robin, however, it comes in a blinding flash which almost causes him to lose his senses. Hawthorne creates this vision in his brilliant description of Molineux at the climactic moment:

He was an elderly man, of large and majestic person, and strong, square features, betokening a steady soul; but steady as it was, his enemies had found means to shake it. His face was pale as death, and far more ghastly; the broad forehead was contracted in his agony, so that his eyebrows formed one grizzled line; his eyes were red and wild, and the foam hung white upon his quivering lip. His whole frame was agitated by a quick and continual tremor, which his pride strove to quell, even in those circumstances of overwhelming humiliation. But perhaps the bitterest pang of all was when his eyes met those of Robin; for he evidently knew him on the instant, as the youth stood witnessing the foul disgrace of a head grown gray in honor.[18]

To correct the traumatic effects of this experience, Robin bursts into mad, unrestrained laughter. At the end of the story it is uncertain as to whether or not Robin will ever be able to recover from this trauma, whether or not reality has proved too much for him.

Many symbols serve effectively to highlight irony and paradox. The Mississippi River, of course, symbolizes the paradox of an ambiguous god of nature. The exhumed graves in both *The Adventures of Huckleberry Finn* and *Intruder in the Dust* symbolize the paradox that only through the dead can some of the riddles of the living be solved. The canoe in *An American Tragedy* symbolizes the irony of Clyde's reversal of fortune. His meeting Roberta in a canoe seems to indicate the promise of happiness and fulfillment for the distraught youth, but his intimacies with her eventually prove his undoing, and the irony reaches full circle through the fateful incident in the canoe in which he plans to murder Roberta. Henry Fleming's wound symbolizes the paradox of courage acquired through cowardice. The electric light bulb in *Martin Eden* symbolizes the revolutionary progress of man through history. As a symbol it adds ironic significance to the brutal fist fight of Martin and Cheese Face in the rays of its light. The ships *The Indomitable* and *The Rights of Man* in *Billy Budd* ironically symbolize the reverse qualities for which they are named. On the former absolute morality is defeated, and on the latter the rights of men are shamelessly violated. Students ought to be able to draw out many more ironic symbols from these works.

Most students react negatively to teachers who would teach literature didactically with a particular view of morality in mind. Students would rather draw moral conclusions on their own, independent of the teacher's interpretation, and from these conclusions derive norms of behavior and conduct through which they can order their lives and develop their personalities. All good literature concerns itself with

[18] Nathaniel Hawthorne, "My Kinsman, Major Molineux," in Foerster, p. 617.

morality, and can in many ways be instrumental in helping to improve character and in promoting the notion of the good life. The more sensitive the student becomes to the nuances of irony and paradox, the more able he is to realize these desired objectives by perceiving truth more fully. The person with a refined sense of irony and paradox is more likely to avoid the disappointments and disasters of life which arrogance and pride often bring in their wake. Shelley's poem "Ozymandias" illustrates this point most effectively. Like Huck Finn and Ike McCaslin, the student might attain the humility necessary to accept himself for what he really is, and gain the judgement to distinguish evil from good in his own experiences.

5

Romanticism and realism as style

A knowledge of American transcendentalism is crucial to an understanding of the romanticism which characterizes so much of American fiction. The leading exponents of the doctrine of transcendentalism in American literature are Thoreau and Emerson, the former being its practitioner primarily and its philosopher secondarily, the latter its philosopher primarily and its practitioner secondarily. The basic tenets of transcendentalism are comprehensively expounded in Thoreau's *Walden* and "Civil Disobedience," and Emerson's "Nature," "The American Scholar," and "Self-Reliance." These works, along with others which will be mentioned in the course of this discussion, should constitute an essential core of readings for the teacher who would desire a broad understanding of the concept of romanticism.

Many of the basic principles of romantic transcendentalism as enunciated by Thoreau and Emerson find expression in the content and style of some of the works under discussion here. Perhaps the most important principle of transcendentalism is that the individual as a sovereign entity takes precedence over the group. In this sense he becomes something of a god, a law unto himself, capable of ordering and directing his own destiny with little help from others. He epitomizes the inner-directed man at his best—a unique and totally fulfilled person, a man of thought as well as action, as interested in ideas as he is in things, a creature able to turn every moment of his life into a vital, meaningful experience, and in so doing to set an example for all men. He has humility, yet he is proud and self-respecting. He is the ideal man that all men should strive to become.

Transcendental man is able and willing to confront life and to incur the risks involved in immersing himself in the flux of experience. His career can be plotted on an experiential continuum through which he develops and continually renews himself. A reasonable, rational man, yet he relies heavily for guidance on an almost infallible intuition which he has acquired in the course of his development; he is ever on the lookout for unique and original experience; he puts little stock in the values received through custom and tradition; he puts a high value on the flash insight, and sees merit in acting spontaneously in a given situation; he has unshakable faith in man's ability to progress, and sees in the world of nature about him the wherewithal and the inspiration through which progress can be realized.

Another type of ideal man is classical man, who attains his fulfillment in a manner quite different from the romantic man of transcendentalism. The classical attitude is best summed up in the writings of such authors as Matthew Arnold and Cardinal Newman, T. E. Hulme ("Romanticism and Classicism"), and the neo-humanists of the twentieth century like Paul Elmer More, Irving Babbitt, Robert Maynard Hutchins, and Jacques Barzun. Gilbert Highet in *The Art of Teaching* and Richard Hofstadter in *Anti-Intellectualism in American Life* articulate most clearly the classical attitude.

Classical man differs from romantic man in that the former does not glorify or deify the human personality. The individual is a relative, not an absolute, entity to the classicist. Like romantic man, classical man is able to control his own destiny, but unlike romantic man he has a sense of tradition direction which causes him to respect customs and institutions. His humility and self-respect derive from a sense of noblesse oblige, rather than from a sense of his own absolute worth in comparison with other men. He is an aristocrat, whereas romantic man is a democrat. He does not immerse himself so readily in the flux of uncertain experience as does romantic man. Though he believes in human progress, he is less inclined than romantic man to believe that humans are completely capable of effecting their own progress. Rather, he sees often serious limitations in man which he associates with the Christian conception of original sin or the Greek conception of hubris. Though he believes in the reconstruction of experience in unique and original ways, he insists that this be achieved through building upon the received culture of the past, as does T. S. Eliot in "Tradition and the Individual Talent." He differs, too, from romantic man in that he does not glorify or deify nature in any pantheistic way. Rather he approaches nature objectively, even clinically, and sometimes indifferently. Thus he does not indulge in the kinds of emotionalism and subjectivism that so often characterize romantic man. Finally, classical man, unlike romantic man, relies more on reason to order his experience than on uncontrolled intuition. In sum, one might say that romantic man is more liberal and revolutionary in his outlook, and classical man more conservative and restrained in his.

Ultimately, romanticism and classicism are idealistic concepts, but they are idealistic in different, even opposing, ways. The principles that characterize romanticism and classicism can apply either to persons, themes, or the structures of works of art. That is, an idealistic person may be either romantic or classical in outlook, or a combination of both; and a work of art may be structured according to the same principles of romanticism and classicism that define character. The concern of this chapter will be with these principles in the context of character and theme. In the chapter on structure as a function of style these principles will apply to the structures of works of fiction.

When carried to extremes, the principles of romanticism and classicism can result in undesirable traits of character and personality, distortion of theme, and structural deficiencies in works of art. Beatniks and other bohemians overdo romanticism; aristocratic snobs and pedants overdo classicism. Overdone romanticism leads to inconsistency, instability, and disorder of style; overdone classicism leads to dogmatism, rigidity, and inflexibility of style. The former is anarchistic; the latter totalitarian and tyrannical.

It would be virtually impossible to categorize the content or style of any fictional work as either totally romantic or classical. Except for the obvious difference that the romantic style is characterized by egocentrism, emotionalism, and spontaneous intuitive insights to a much greater extent than is classicism, both romanticism and classicism aim for the same ideal: ultimate truth and a viable philosophy of human fulfillment. In this sense, paradoxically, they perhaps have more in common than they have in contrast. Romanticism and classicism, therefore, are not diametrically opposed outlooks. But, as idealistic outlooks, they both are diametrically opposed to realism, an outlook which is essentially anti-idealistic. In most of the works of this discussion, the principles of romanticism apply more readily in interpreting content than

do the principles of classicism. Thus, character and theme in this dis
cussion will for the most part be interpreted in the light of romanticisn
versus realism, with references to classicism whenever appropriate.

As an anti-idealist, the realist objects to romanticism on the ground
that it concerns itself to an unreasonable degree with things as on
would *like* them to be or as they *ought* to be, rather than with things a
they really *are*. The realist argues that the romanticist sets up ideal
that are impossible of attainment in human experience, that the roman
ticist is often given to the most pernicious kind of wishful thinking whicl
does great damage to the cause of truth in art. The realist for the mos
part rejects the emotionalism, intuitionism, and sentimentalism of th
romantic. He prefers to examine the human situation with the un
clouded vision of a camera and the clinical objectivity of the researcl
scientist. To the realist the only valid data at one's disposal consists o
that which is gained through the senses, *a posteriori*, untainted by pre
judice or chimerical ideals. Realism attempts to give the lie to roman
ticism through a devastating process of debunking.

Much of American fiction is realistic in content and style. In th
works of many authors, of course, a combination of the techniques o
both romanticism and realism may be employed. American fictioi
from the last quarter of the nineteenth century to the present is pre
dominantly realistic. Writers such as Howells and Crane wrote in ;
manner quite different from the popular Victorian and Gilded Ag
writers of the times who presented life and manners through a romanti
haze. Later in the nineteenth century and in the early twentieth century
realistic writers represented by such men as Dreiser, Norris, London
and Sinclair went beyond ordinary realism to a point which is properl
classed as naturalism, a more virulent opponent of romanticism thai
the comparatively tame realism of Howells and Crane.[1]

Emile Zola sums up the philosophy of naturalism in his comment;
on the experimental novel. To him the essence of naturalism reside
in determinism, which

dominates everything. . . . Man is not alone; he lives in society, in a socia
condition; and consequently, for us novelists, this social condition unceasingl
modifies the phenomena. Indeed our great study is just there, in the reciproca
effects of society on the individual and the individual on society. For th

---

[1] In *Maggie, Girl of the Streets* Crane is much closer to the naturalistic style than he is ii
The Red Badge of Courage.

physiologist, the exterior and interior conditions are purely chemical and physical, and this aids him in finding the laws which govern them easily. . . . From this we shall see that we can act upon the social conditions, in acting upon the phenomena of which we have made ourselves master in man. And this is what constitutes the experimental novel: to possess a knowledge of the mechanism of the phenomena inherent in man, to show the machinery of his intellectual and sensory manifestations, under the influence of heredity and environment.[2]

Two American authors have written brilliantly on the phenomena of naturalism. No teacher who desires a deeper understanding of naturalism should fail to read Malcolm Cowley's "A Natural History of American Naturalism," and Joseph Wood Krutch's *The Modern Temper.*

Cowley describes and explains naturalism with perhaps more detachment and objectivity than does Krutch. His main point is that "The effect of naturalism as a doctrine is to subtract from literature the whole notion of human responsibility."[3] The guiding principle of Naturalism is blind, omnipotent force which transcends human efforts and makes of man a helpless pawn of circumstance.[4] Such is the effect in Frank Norris's *The Pit.* For to Norris, "Wheat was not a grain improved by men from various wild grasses and grown by men to meet human needs; it was an abstract and elemental force like gravity."[5] In their attempt to achieve the ultimate in realism "The naturalists as a group not only based their work on current scientific theories, but tried to copy scientific methods in planning their novels."[6] They functioned as clinicians observing the behavior patterns of "human insects" that served as laboratory specimens, and they reduced to shambles the conventional notions of orthodox Christianity and the theories of human perfectibility so passionately expounded by the transcendentalists.

Krutch displays a classicist's bias in his critique of naturalism. He decries the fact that the naturalists have alienated man from God, and have reduced him to an animal state by denying the values affirmed

[2] Emile Zola, *The Experimental Novel and Other Essays* (New York: Haskell House, 1964), pp. 18, 20–21.
[3] Malcolm Cowley, "A Natural History of American Naturalism," in Aldridge, p. 374.
[4] *Ibid.,* p. 370.
[5] *Ibid.,* p. 373.
[6] *Ibid.,* p. 380.

by tradition and Revelation, and by shattering the norms of absolute morality.[7] Thus living in a hostile and indifferent universe, man suffers the agonies of "Quiet desperation, that famous phrase which Thoreau used to describe the mood of the average man . . . the result of an impotent protest against the realization that he is playing the animal' part without being blessed with the animal's unconscious acquiescence."[8] Despite his anti-naturalistic views, however, Krutch is not altogether convinced that the classicist's position is absolutely tenable. For he admits the dilemma that "The proposition that life is a science is intellectually indefensible; the proposition that life is an art is pragmatically impossible."[9] Nevertheless, throughout his discussion Krutch does betray a much greater sympathy for the latter proposition than he does for the former.

In *The Adventures of Huckleberry Finn*, perhaps to a greater degree than in any other work considered here, the principles of romanticism and realism are equally evident. This manifests itself in subtle and complex ways. Perhaps the most obvious of these ways is revealed through comparing and contrasting Huck and Tom both in what they are, and in how what they are influences what they do and what they believe. Both are romantics, but in different ways. Tom's romanticism is irredeemably farcical and fantastic. He is impractical and silly, and given to grandiosity and bombast to a degree that some critics find offensive and in bad taste aesthetically. This is most evident in the beginning and ending portions of the book, which contrast remarkably with the middle portion. Thomas Arthur Gullason sees this as a "romantic-realist quarrel," which

is part of Mark Twain's conscious plot against the real antagonist of the novel, Tom Sawyer. He returns at the end because, like Huck, he is a major character who needs to be set in a final position. The story has come a long way. . . [But] Tom remains the child of the first chapters. . . . His life has been a continuous lie . . . Tom himself is wounded when Jim does escape—that epitomizes his romantic nonsense.[10]

---

[7] Joseph Wood Krutch, *The Modern Temper* (New York: Harcourt, Brace & World, 1956), p. 18.

[8] *Ibid.*, p. 24.

[9] *Ibid.*, p. 115.

[10] Thomas Arthur Gullason, "The Fatal Ending of *Huckleberry Finn*," in Bradley, *Huck Finn*, p. 360.

Huck, on the other hand, is a romantic in a more sensible way. V. S. Pritchett sees a romantic facet in Huck's nature. He suggests that Huck, like other characters of American fiction who are strongly affected by nostalgia, and like rebels longing for a master or a spiritual home, not only harks back to something lost in the past, but also looks forward to the tragedy of a lost future.[11]

Huck's romanticism takes even more positive forms. He has a deep love for nature, as evidenced by his reverence for the Mississippi River, and when necessary knows how to use his imagination to advantage. He displays the same flair for drama and playacting as Tom when he escapes from the cabin and feigns his own murder by spreading the blood of a pig on the earth. Unlike Tom, however, he would not do all this for its own sake. Rather, he does it to accomplish his symbolic death and to make his break from society. He is a romantic, too, in that he does not hate persons who are evil and who mistreat him. He refuses to become a cynic and a pessimist, and finds something worthy of sympathy in everyone, even Pap and the Duke and the Dauphin.

Huck differs from Tom, too, in that he is a realist. He is much more mature and perceptive than Tom. He gauges situations correctly and interprets human beings for what they really are. He entertains no delusions about the nature of the human condition, and makes no attempt to escape from or dismiss his uncomfortable insights through fantasy or rationalization. Yet his realism is tempered by just enough romanticism to keep him from becoming a naturalist.

As a novelist Mark Twain reveals a realist's bias. Though he applies the principles of romanticism in his content and style, his attitude toward romanticism is basically satirical. For the most part, however, the satire is good-humored and not vicious. Twain pokes fun at Tom's quixotic attitudes, and at his realiance upon authority and tradition as the fountainheads of truth. In the Phelps Farm incidents, which constitute roughly the last one-fourth of the work, Twain takes perhaps his most vicious cut at romanticism by presenting it in caricature. Unfortunately, this farcical style detracts considerably from the esthetic merit of the presentation. In lampooning the morbid sentimentalism and necrophilia of Emmaline Grangerford, however, Twain does succeed in creating high humor, although it is of the "sick" variety.

Though he does present the seamier sides of human nature, one

V. S. Pritchett, in Bradley, *Huck Finn*, p. 307.

cannot properly classify Twain as a naturalist. This is so because his humor serves to take the sting out of the underlying morbidity and cynicism of the work. It would be a profitable pedagogical exercise for students to examine in conjunction with *The Adventures of Huckleberry Finn* works like Twain's "The Man Who Corrupted Hadleyburg" and "The Mysterious Stranger," in which he makes an obvious attempt to write in a naturalistic style. In trying to write like a naturalist however, Twain gets out of his element. He rants and raves and overstates his case. His anger is unrestrained, his cynicism childish and unsophisticated. Without humor, which is his forte, his style tends to lose much of its force and vigor.

The Red Badge of Courage is a naturalistic novel in that it makes much of the idea that man is a cipher in the universe. This, of course is in direct opposition to the Emersonian view of nature as a beneficent entity which generously provides the means for man to lead a good and proper life, if only he would have the courage and the self-reliance to trust his natural impulses and intuitions. Henry Fleming sees nature differently—as an indifferent force totally unconcerned with and detached from the concerns of men at war: "It was surprising that Nature had gone tranquilly on with her golden process in the midst of so much devilment."[12] Even more surprising to Henry is his shocking realization of his own insignificance, of the utter puniness of his ego which during his moments of self-deception has inflated to undue proportions: "He craved a power that would enable him to make a world-sweeping gesture and brush all back. His impotency appeared to him and made his rage into that of a driven beast."[13] Nature in *The Red Badge of Courage* is the nature that Harry Hartwick speaks of in his evaluation of the naturalistic style in American fiction. It is an amoral self-running machine without direction. The only consistency it has is that it tends to favor the strong over the weak. If a man's animal impulses and physical reflexes occur at the right time and under the right circumstances he may overcome nature and survive. Survival thus becomes a matter of probability and chance.[14]

But, with all its naturalistic motifs, *The Red Badge of Courage* is very

[12] Crane, p. 35.

[13] *Ibid.*, p. 32.

[14] Harry Hartwick, *The Foreground of American Fiction* (New York: American Book Co. 1934), p. 18–19.

a romantic novel in many ways. The better side of human nature reveals itself in many incidents and situations. There is a transcendental quality in the "subtle brotherhood of man" tha the soldiers experience among themselves. They are often generous to one another in times of stress. Henry displays a humane concern for Jim Conklin, who eventually dies of his wounds, and Henry himself is given the most tender care and attention when he returns to his regiment. Henry's mother, unlike the mothers of Sparta whom Henry has read about in the romantic tales of Homer, displays a concern for his well-being which resounds in high pathos, and which is in no way naturalistic or overly sentimental. The closing paragraphs of the work are saturated with the transcendental spirit. Here Crane overstates Henry's attainment and fulfillment in a gush of rhetoric which is almost Emersonian, and somewhat out of tune with the more negative and pessimistic statements found elsewhere in the work.

The Catcher in the Rye is a romantic novel in a Rousseaulian sense. Robert O. Bowen observes that "The story provides a nostalgia for childhood as a defense against the insights of maturity as though the adult world were by nature evil and miserable."[15] Indeed, like all romantics who desire a return to a happier state, Holden is destined to disillusionment, and is totally incapable, too, of making the transition from childhood to adulthood. He cannot endure the risks that such a transition would entail. All his strategy is misdirected in his efforts to achieve the security of childhood, but, ironically, his efforts serve only to compound his insecurity. His desire to be the "catcher" is in reality a symptom of a more deeply rooted problem—his inability to return to the security of childhood, and to put to rest the uncertainty and the distractions of the experiences in which he finds himself so inextricably enmeshed. He is enough of a realist, however, to know that he cannot return to the secure state of his childhood, and must thus settle for a lesser state by identifying with those who he would rather be, children in a state of innocence. Another symptom reveals itself in his desire to live a wordless life with Sally Hayes in a cabin camp, away from all the distractions of the adult world, and in the security he gains whenever he is with his sister Phoebe.

The Catcher in the Rye is a realistic novel in that it honestly presents to the reader Holden's true predicament. It is a naturalistic novel in

[15] Bowen, p. 52.

that it depicts many depressing realities of the human situation. Salinger strikes a happy balance in his employment of the romantic, realistic, and naturalistic styles. Holden may be summed up as a romantic character portrayed in a naturalistic setting.

In *Billy Budd* both romanticism and naturalism are operative. But Melville's naturalism is of an entirely different kind from the naturalism of Crane, Dreiser, and others. Melville, like these authors, admits to blind forces at work in human affairs, but he attributes them to more than just the accidents of heredity and environment. Melville's outlook is Calvinistic. He raises theological questions which are ultimately unanswerable. In effect, he quarrels with God: "Man's fault, says Melville, is God's fault."[16] To the naturalists of Dreiser's class God is entirely out of contention in human affairs.

Of all the young heroes considered here, none exemplify the romantic ideal of the noble savage as well as Billy Budd does. Through Billy "Melville attempts to portray the native purity and nobility of the uncorrupted man."[17] His innate goodness does him no good, however, in a world mysteriously controlled by the powers of evil. For, though "Billy may be as blameless as Oedipus of any evil intention, yet a malign fate, working upon his inevitable limitations as a human being, brings it about that he commits in fact a capital crime."[18] Essentially, Melville was not a transcendentalist. He believed in evil as a positive and absolute force, not as a negative and relative force as did Emerson. Nevertheless, like the transcendentalists, he did believe in the inviolability of the human spirit, and the affirmative nature of man's faith in a final resolution of the dilemmas and contradictions that have bedeviled man throughout history. Billy's situation dramatizes this belief. In this respect, too, Melville differs from the typical naturalists, whose cynicism rules out the paradoxical possibility that evil may ultimately be transformed into good.

Dreiser's *An American Tragedy* is a novel that truly typifies the American naturalistic outlook. H. L. Mencken sums up Dreiser's main attitude as a naturalist: "He would make us specks in the insentient

---

[16] Lawrence Thompson, *Melville's Quarrel with God* (Princeton: Princeton University Press, 1952), p. 379.

[17] Raymond M. Weaver, *Herman Melville, Mariner and Mystic* (New York: Pageant Books, 1960), p. 381.

[18] Newton Arvin, *Herman Melville: A Critical Biography* (New York: 1950), p. 297.

embryo of some gigantic Presence . . . he would interpret the whole phenomenon of life as no more than an appearance, a nightmare of some unseen sleeper or of men themselves, an 'uncanny blur of nothing' in Euripedes' phrase."[19] Although Dreiser would argue that heredity and environment in the main are to blame for Clyde's misfortunes, he would be hard pressed to explain why Clyde did not inherit his parents' piety, humility, and simplicity, and why so many others, with fewer advantages than Clyde, are yet able to rise above confining environment and live happy, productive lives. Dreiser, of course, believed, too, in mysterious organic forces operative within a person which cause him to behave in a predetermined manner. These "chemisms," as he called them, are the equivalent of Melville's conception of Fate, or a secularized version of the orthodox Christian conception of original sin.

Studs Lonigan and Clyde Griffiths share many traits in common. Studs, even more than Clyde, has advantages in life which should make it possible for him to attain happiness and fulfillment. But, his basic selfishness and lack of concern for others prevent him from achieving these desired ends. Both Clyde and Studs strive desperately to attain happiness and fulfillment, "a place in the sun," but the means they use are morally improper. They seem automatically doomed to failure in their desperate attempts by their employment of unwise or immoral means. And, both youths seem to feel that their failures are caused more by forces outside themselves than by forces from within. They cannot accept the major portion of the responsibility for their own destinies. Like little Davie, one of the more "knowledgeable" characters in *Studs Lonigan*, they would argue in defense of themselves the naturalist's argument that lesbians are lesbians because "they're born that way, or they are made that way because of something that happens in their life."[20] But not because they really choose to be that way.

In *Look Homeward, Angel* Eugene Gant epitomizes the romantic temperament. A raging inferno of emotion and subjectivism, he craves fame, the love of women, and high achievement in the world. The world about him is naturalistic, however. He suffers the disillusionment and pangs of unrequited love; he has to endure the disgust of his mother's crass materialism; he has to watch his brothers Steve and

[19] H. L. Mencken, *A Book of Prefaces* (New York: Alfred A. Knopf, Inc., 1917), in Aldridge, p. 398.
[20] James T. Farrell, *Studs Lonigan* (New York: Vanguard, 1960), p. 374.

Ben engage in a brutal and vicious fist fight; he has to experience at first hand the unsavory sights and sounds of the Norfolk Navy Yard. Like his unstable father, Eugene "had looked much on pain and evil, and remained a fantasist of the Ideal. . . . Again and again he had been bogged in the gray slough of factuality."[21]

Two novels in which the characters move from the illusions of romanticism to the delusions of reality are *This Side of Paradise* and *Martin Eden*. One can trace in detail Amory Blaine's movements from a starry-eyed romantic to a cynic, nihilist, and atheist, and Martin Eden's descent from romanticism to realism to eventual suicide.

In *A Separate Peace* Gene Forrester's sense of nostalgia serves to put into correct perspective his experiences of fifteen years earlier while a student at Devon Preparatory School. With this new perspective he is able to see reality with an intensity that was impossible in his youth. In *The Bear*, Faulkner combines, as he does in so many other of his works, idealistic romanticism with cynical naturalism. One has only to imagine what the work would become without the transcendental qualities which Ike McCaslin and Sam Fathers bring to it—indeed, nothing but a gothic tale of violence and rapine.

A distinguishing feature of the realistic-naturalistic style is found in the author's use of language which attempts to transcribe faithfully the actual experiences that the characters undergo. Thus one often finds in this style (which is similar to Imagism) an intense preoccupation on the part of the author with amassing a plethora of detail in the manner of a research scientist who collects more than enough facts to prove a hypothesis. Dreiser, for example, illustrates this technique in his photographic description of the prison in which Clyde is confined. By meticulously describing the atmosphere of the prison, the criminal backgrounds of the inmates, and the dimming of the lights during an electrocution, Dreiser intensifies the naturalistic horror he is trying to convey. Farrell vividly re-creates the atmosphere of Chicago of World War One and the 1920's through his detailed depiction of news reels, headlines, and social activities such as the famous dance marathon.

[21] Thomas Wolfe, *Look Homeward, Angel* (New York: Charles Scribner's Sons, 1952), p. 325.

Jack London in describing Martin's fight with Cheese Face and the pains that Martin takes to drown himself is at his naturalistic best. Reality is enhanced, too, by the author's faithful transcription of the dialect and idiom of the characters in their respective environments. This is done most effectively by Twain, Salinger, Faulkner, and Crane.

Romantic transcendentalism, taken to its extreme, would argue that the human will is *all* in the determination of human destiny. This attitude would make of man a kind of god with the power to control substantially his own fate. Naturalism, on the other hand, taken to its extreme, would argue that the human will is inconsequential in the determination of human destiny. This attitude would make of man a kind of pawn subject to the overpowering influences of instinct, heredity, environment, or whim. In examining the situations and the problems of the young heroes considered here, teachers and students would be well advised to try to determine just how responsible a character is for his actions, and how much he is to be relieved of responsibility in a given case. This problem is best treated in the light of tragedy, and will be discussed more fully in the next chapter.

It is probably easier to explain the differences between realism and naturalism to students than it is to explain the differences between realism and romanticism. The former task is easier because naturalism for all practical purposes is nothing more than realism with a strong flavor of cynicism and determinism. The latter task is complicated by the fact that, properly speaking, there are several different kinds of romanticism, each unique in its own right. For instance, there is the Rousseaulian kind which is characterized by overdone sentimentalism and nostalgia; the Shelleyan-Byronic kind which emphasizes the egotricity of the nonconforming, rebelling hero; the Keatsian-Whitmanian kind which emphasizes the primacy of sense experience; the Wordsworthian-Coleridgian kind which gives great emphasis to the materials of the past, in contrast to the Emersonian kind, which looks more to the present and the future. In this discussion Emersonian romanticism seems most to apply to the works under consideration in providing a contrast with realism, although the other "romanticisms," too, enjoy some claim as alternatives of style. One would have to agree with George Winchester Stone, who states, "The important thing for a secondary school pupil is not to know the dictionary definition of romanticism, but to understand what there is about certain kinds of reading that makes romanticism a useful word for him."[22] In any case, the terms used in this discussion are relative and elusive, and subject often to careful qualification.

[22] Stone, p. 61.

6

Tragedy and comedy as style

The tragic spirit is possible only in a non-naturalistic context. The romantic and especially the classical points of view lend themselves most suitably to an expression of the tragic spirit. Malcolm Cowley in his critique on naturalism speaks to this point most convincingly:

To say that man is a beast of prey or a collection of chemical compounds omits most of man's special nature; it is a metaphor, not a scientific statement. . . . This scientific weakness of naturalism involves a still greater literary weakness, for it leads to a conception of man that makes it impossible for naturalistic authors to write in a tragic spirit. They can write about crimes, suicides, disasters, the terrifying and the grotesque; but even the most powerful of their novels and plays are case histories rather than tragedies in the classical sense. Tragedy is affirmation of man's importance; it is the 'imitation of noble action' in Aristotle's phrase; and the naturalists are unable to believe in human nobility.[1]

True tragedy is impossible without a recognition of the importance of man in the scheme of the universe. Joseph Wood Krutch, a classicist, views tragedy as "essentially an expression, not of despair, but of triumph over despair and of confidence in the value of human life."[2] For "every real tragedy, however tremendous it may be, is an affirmation of faith in life, a declaration that even if God is not in his Heaven, then at least man is in his world."[3] Krutch bewails the fact that naturalism has stifled the tragic spirit in most modern art. To him, "The death of tragedy is like the death of love, one of those emotional fatalities as the result of which the human as distinguished from the natural world grows more and more a desert.'[4]

[1] Cowley, in Aldridge, p. 385.
[2] Krutch, *Modern Temper*, p. 84.
[3] *Ibid.*, p. 86.
[4] *Ibid.*, p. 97.

The young student must see that there is a vast difference between tragedy and misfortune, between the tragic hero and the pathetic hero who are represented by these qualities respectively. In effect, tragedy is suffering and misfortune realized on a grand scale, suffering and misfortune whose effects ramify to boundless proportions. The tragic hero must be made to stand for universal man more than particular man, and he must be involved in an action in which high stakes are at issue. He must be able to enlist one's respect and admiration by virtue of his nobility and dignity, and to enlist one's sympathy by virtue of his failings as an imperfect human being. The action that he is involved in must raise profound, though ultimately unanswerable questions as to the nature of truth, justice, good, and evil. Finally, in keeping with the spirit of tragedy, the artist must employ elevated language appropriate to the gravity of the tragic situation. Except for a consideration of the necessary qualities of the tragic hero which he treats in other parts of the "Poetics," Aristotle defines tragedy as

an imitation of an action that is serious, complete, and of a certain magnitude; in language embellished with each kind of artistic ornament, the several kinds being found in separate parts of the play; in the form of action, not of narrative; through pity and fear effecting the proper purgation of these emotions.[5]

Throughout the "Poetics" Aristotle makes much of the fact that only certain men are capable of the tragic experience. With some qualifications this is quite true. First, a man must be in such a position of authority or responsibility that his decisions and actions will profoundly affect the destinies of many men; that is, possibly alter the course of human history to some degree. Second, he must be capable of knowing clearly right from wrong, and of suffering acutely whenever he violates morality. Third, he must be willing to risk eternal damnation or utter loss as a result of his misjudgments. Fourth, he must always lose in a worldly sense, but he must always win in the sense that he has demonstrated to the world his absolute ability to assert his will, however wrong his choice of action may be, and however ineffectual his will. Fifth, there must be some factor (or factors) in his situation which serves to exonerate him from absolute responsibility for his actions. The true tragic hero must fulfill all five of these qualifications to a significant degree. If he does not, the chances are that he is a pathetic hero instead.

[5] Aristotle, "Poetics," in Butcher, p. 23.

Arthur Miller argues that the common man is as capable of the tragic experience as the true tragic hero outlined above: "Common man is as apt a subject for tragedy in its highest sense as kings were."[6] And in a sense Miller is correct: "The commonest of men may take that stature to the extent of his willingness to throw all he has into the contest, the battle to secure his rightful place in the world. . . . The possibility of victory must be there in tragedy . . . the belief . . . in the perfectibility of man."[7] However, Miller does not argue directly that his Willy Loman of *Death of a Salesman* is a true tragic character, but he seems to imply as much just the same. Certainly, Loman does suffer as excruciatingly as, say, Macbeth or Oedipus, who are more properly classed as tragic characters. But, in scarcely any other way does he compare with these characters. The student who examines Willy Loman's situation closely has to conclude that Loman lacks the tragic grandeur of Macbeth or Oedipus. He is a petty, mean, contemptuous person. Unlike Macbeth, he lies and cheats without compunction. He lacks Macbeth's sense of conscience and his noble courage. He does not, like Macbeth, take really daring risks. His ambition to be "liked" is his predominant motivation. Like Clyde Griffiths and Studs Lonigan, he views comfort and security as the highest of attainable ends. His suicide is an act of cowardice, not a dignified solution to an insurmountable problem. He lacks completely Oedipus' personal integrity and willingness to bear responsibility for his unconscious transgressions. His intense unawareness of self and reality properly classifies him as the epitome of mid-twentieth-century naturalistic man, a human pawn whose will is utterly powerless to influence his destiny.

In all well-conceived tragedy there is a balanced interplay between will and fate; that is, between those forces one can control and those forces over which one is powerless. If this interplay gets out of balance and will predominates, the tragic sense is lost because man approaches godlike proportions and has the potential to ward off all misfortune. If fate predominates, the tragic sense is lost because man is deprived of his ability and his freedom to direct his destiny, and is thus not responsible for whatever may befall him. The pathetic hero is often the victim of fate and accident. The true tragic hero applies his entire

[6] Arthur Miller, "Tragedy and the Common Man," in Brown, *A Quarto of Modern Literature*, p. 537.

[7] *Ibid.*, pp. 537–38.

energies in an effort to ward off fate. He refuses to succumb to over-whelming odds. His energies may be misdirected, but he applies them just the same because of his faith in his act of will. He is truly willing to risk all, to confront whatever is his lot, and to assume full responsibility for his action. His self-deceptions are the result of ignorance or lack of insight, not rationalization. We may pity him for his recklessness and foolishness, but we admire him for his intense sense of self-awareness, and his sense of the freedom that he has to defy fate. He may not disprove the principles of naturalism by his actions, but his attempt to do so gains him merit and respect. Even though men like Macbeth and Ahab bring more evil and destruction in their wakes than do men like Clyde Griffiths and Willy Loman, they are yet more admirable because, through their intense commitment to the act of will, they dignify man by suggesting that the will when directed properly has an immense potential for good, though in their cases this potential is not realized. The tragedy of Macbeth and Ahab lies in their willful employment of evil means to effect a desirable end, and their partial inability to see their evil means for what they really are. To a degree this is true, too, of Loman and Griffiths. These two differ markedly from the former, however, in that they are not prepared to take full responsibility for their actions. They delude themselves by assigning responsibility for their misfortunes to forces from without.

An understanding of tragedy is a necessary element of a true liberal education. Burton observes: "Tragedy, after all, makes suffering bearable by making it understandable, and understanding of tragedy should be an aim of the senior high school literature program."[8] Despite the fact "that tragedy portrays a self-division and self-waste of spirit, or a division of spirit involving conflict and waste,"[9] it yet invests man with dignity. For "Tragic art predicates the *special* universality of man's capacity for greatness of soul and mind in spite of his *hamartia* or the flaw in his nature."[10] Tragedy educates man to rise above his petty concerns, and to share vicariously the universal experiences of mankind. For

Tragedy involves our capacity to feel for others and fear for ourselves, too, by knowing that we share in their humanity and that they share in ours. . . .

[8] Burton, p. 10.

[9] A. C. Bradley, "Hegel's Theory of Tragedy," in Anne and Henry Paolucci, eds., *Hegel on Tragedy* (Garden City: Doubleday 1962), p. 381.

[10] John Gassner, "Aristotelian Literary Criticism," in Butcher, p. lxvi.

Tragic art is for those who are not merely mature. It does not express itself to the storm trooper any more than to the sentimentalist.[11]

Tragedy educates, too, by making man more sensitive to the demands of morality, and in serving to refine one's sense of irony so as to acquire the judgment to avoid misfortune in one's own life. Often the tragic hero's flaw lies in his inability to distinguish appearances from realities. And in all true tragedy morality cannot be violated with impunity. Justice wreaks a frightful vengeance.

Tragedy provides pleasure. "The delight of tragedy proceeds from our consciousness of fiction; if we thought murders and treasons real they would please us no more."[12] We can put up with the horror of tragedy because we are detached from the actual experience of the horror. This detachment is a function of the aesthetic distance which all good art provides for its participants. We become involved vicariously and identify with the tragic hero often more in sympathy than in empathy, and the involvement is a painless one because we are not in reality held responsible for the tragic hero's action. Yet we judge the morality of his action and probably gain added delight from the knowledge that it is not our action. We may even feel superior to the tragic hero, and take pride in ourselves for having the wisdom not to get into his situation.

Much has been written of Aristotle's concept of catharsis or psychic purification with regard to tragedy. Aristotle seems to say in the "Poetics" that it is the purpose of tragedy to inspire in us pity and fear, the affective states created through the process of identification with the tragic hero.[13] Through the excitation of these emotions one can release them more effectively, and take pleasure from their release in the same way that one can gain delight from eating after prolonging hunger. The relief, which occurs after the resolution of the tragedy, is savored in direct proportion to the tension which preceded it. Thus, emotion is excited in order that it may be pleasurably released.[14] This homeopathic outcome is achieved by "curing emotion by means of an emotion like in kind but not identical."[15] Perhaps the best way to explain this

---

[11] *Ibid.*, pp. xlii–xliii.
[12] Samuel Johnson, in Dewey, p. 96.
[13] Butcher, p. 263.
[14] *Ibid.*, pp. 245–47.
[15] *Ibid.*, p. 248.

phenomenon to the young student is through relating it to the experience he undergoes whenever he watches a suspenseful play. Ordinarily, the student wants his suspense to reach an "unendurable" level so that he may take delight in its dissipation. Although this analogy is a vast oversimplification of what Aristotle probably really meant, it has enough similarity with catharsis to have pedagogical value.

A. C. Bradley makes a subtle observation relative to the nature of tragedy which the teacher may use to great profit in promoting and sustaining a classroom discussion:

The essentially tragic fact is the self division and intestinal warfare of the ethical substance, not so much the war of good with evil as the war of good with good. Two of these isolated powers face each other, making incompatible demands. The family claims what the state refuses, love requires what honor forbids . . . the claim of each is equally justified; but the right of each is pulled into a wrong, because it ignores the right of the other and demands that absolute sway which belongs to neither alone, but to the whole of which each is but a part.[16]

This statement may be put to good use in a final examination question, also.

Billy Budd is the one work in this discussion which best exemplifies the style of tragedy. It is not Billy who is the tragic figure; rather it is Vere. Billy is an unfortunate victim who has many flaws. He is naive, inarticulate, and passive—hardly the qualities one would expect to find in a true tragic character. As an allegorical figure, however, he dramatizes the tragic fact that the world cannot endure goodness, and he serves to create the occasion for Vere's tragedy to be enacted.

Nor is Claggart a truly tragic character. He is too abstract and too given to evil for its own sake to represent universal man, though he does represent the evil component universally apparent in human nature. As an allegorical figure he dramatizes the tragic fact that evil is a reality in the world of man, and that acts of iniquity are difficult to redeem and atone for through human justice. Both he and Billy represent antithetical absolutes which must of necessity clash, and through this clash present Vere with the dilemma that generates the tragedy.

Critics like Phil Withim, who brand Vere as an immoral coward, fail to see his situation as tragic. And it is only through tragedy that

[16] A. C. Bradley, p. 369.

Vere can be vindicated. The act of will that Withim demands of Vere in the interest of absolute morality seems unreasonable in the light of the realities of human nature and the ways of the world. It asks of a man that he take an absolute position at all costs, even bloodshed, as Thoreau does in "Civil Disobedience." For, "Is there not a sort of blood shed when the conscience is wounded?" [17] But human situations are relative, not absolute. Only in the world of ideas, not things and actions, can an absolute position be taken. And, as an intellectual, Vere is better equipped to deal with ideas than with men and things. This fact adds to the tragedy of his situation. Withim seems to be arguing that the moral doctrine which allows one to choose between the lesser of two evils when one must make a choice, is a sophistry. Rather, he would say, one must always reject evil at all times, under all circumstances, and at all costs. One cannot argue with the nobility of such a view. But in a world complicated by the conflicting demands of morality, it is at best impractical, at worst plausible. Wendell Glick applies Bradley's tragic conception of "the war of good with good" to Vere's situation:

Justice to the individual is not the ultimate loyalty in a complex culture; the stability of the culture has the higher claim, and when the two conflict, justice to the individual must be abrogated to keep the order of society intact.[18]

Furthermore, Vere, like all men, is a victim of evils over which he has no control—evils which have put him in situations not of his own making, situations in which he would rather not be. These evils have existed since the dawn of human history and have begotten other evils which subsequent generations of men have inherited through little fault of their own. The French Revolution was a reaction against the evils of a corrupt aristocratic society. It in time became an evil force, however, which Napoleon used to further his ambitions. The countries that waged war against France had to resort to the evil of impressment which forced men into military service against their wills. It seems that all these evils had to be allowed in order to achieve a higher good. From an idealistic standpoint, however, they should not have been allowed. Billy is doomed by the cumulative force of all these evils, and Vere, in a practical sense, is powerless to prevent his doom because of the need

[17] Thoreau, "Civil Disobedience," in Foerster, p. 548.
[18] Wendell Glick, "Expediency and Absolute Morality in *Billy Budd*," *PMLA*, LXVIII (March, 1953), p. 104.

to fulfill a higher duty, as did Christ, who even though he had the power to prevent his crucifixion, yet committed a suicide of sorts to serve a higher good. As Richard Harter Fogle observes, it is impossible for an unfallen man like Billy to exist for long in a fallen world.[19]

Vere is further exonerated by the fact that he acted sincerely and with no evil intent. Unlike truly non-tragic figures such as Clyde Griffiths and Studs Lonigan, he was not motivated by personal ambition or a desire for comfort or security. Ultimately his actions may have proven unwise or ill-advised (the "might have been" that Melville speaks of), but there is no way to gauge this with certainty. All men are limited in their judgments and their insights. No man ever knows what the ultimate outcome of his action may be. All men do know their own intentions, however, and there is no overpowering evidence to the effect that Vere's intentions were anything but honorable—to his own knowledge or to the knowledge of the reader. Melville seems to solve Vere's problem to his own satisfaction by suggesting that men are incapable of administering perfect justice on earth, and must settle for imperfect justice until the "Last Assizes" when God will finally balance the scales of justice. But, to one who cannot accept Orthodox Christianity or Judaism, this solution is a mystical rationalization, which some men believe that other men will use to shirk their responsibilities and to excuse their immoral behavior.

In is an oversimplification to say that tragedy is serious and comedy is humorous, that the hallmark of tragedy is a disastrous ending, and that of comedy a happy ending. Nevertheless, there are elements of truth in these generalizations, and like all good generalizations that are subjected to suitable qualifiers and disclaimers, they can serve as the foundation on which to build a higher and more sophisticated truth. In his discussion of comedy, Wylie Sypher comments: "Perhaps the most important discovery of modern criticism is the perception that comedy and tragedy are somehow akin."[20] There is a great deal of truth in this somewhat paradoxical statement. Tragedy and comedy differ in that, on the surface, comedy seems far removed from tragedy; a close examination of comedy reveals, however, that beneath the surface there are often very real undercurrents of tragedy; and that humor

[19] Richard Harter Fogle, "*Billy Budd*—Acceptance or Irony," *Tulane Studies in English*, VIII (1958), p. 111.
[20] Sypher, p. 193.

tends to keep them submerged. In this sense true tragedy treats of grave misfortune overtly, while comedy treats of it obliquely and indirectly. It is more difficult to defend the converse proposition that in tragedy there are undercurrents of humor, although the teacher must point out that the tragic author may often provide comic relief scenes (as is done so well in *Hamlet*, *Macbeth*, and *Moby Dick*) to divert the reader momentarily in order that the tragedy can be continued and sustained more effectively.

Tragedy differs from comedy, too, in that "a tragic action needs to convey a sense of destiny, inevitability, and foreordination. . . . Somehow tragedy shows what *must* happen. . . . Unlike tragedy, comedy does not have to guard itself by any logic of inevitability."[21] In other words, the comic artist can be more playful and less serious in his treatment of the human situation.

One sees this difference in *Billy Budd* and *The Adventures of Huckleberry Finn*. In the former, disaster and misfortune are inevitable. Absolute morality has to be violated. Vere has no other course. In the latter, as V. S. Pritchett observes:

Mark Twain obliges you to accept the boy as the humorous norm. Without him the violence of the book would be stark reporting of low life. For if this is a great comic book, it is also a book of terror and brutality.[22]

The comic artist subdues tragedy; ever keeps it in check by laughing at it; tones down its capacity for disaster and misfortune. He by no means destroys it as a reality. He simply presents it in a different perspective, and by effectively making a "fool" of tragedy, he achieves a homeopathetic catharsis, as does the tragic artist. Instead, he cures folly with folly. "For Folly is the natural prey of the Comic, known to it in all her transformations, in every disguise."[23] In comedy there is always the potential for tragedy, but the comic artist never permits this potential to be fully realized. He presents tragedy by presenting

the frailties, follies, and infirmities of human nature, as distinguished from its graver vices or crimes. . . . Its blunders and discords, its imperfect correspondences and adjustments, and that in matters intellectual as well as moral.[24]

[21] *Ibid.*, p. 219.
[22] V. S. Pritchett, "*Huckleberry Finn* and the Cruelty of American Humor," in Bradley, *Huck Finn*, p. 308.
[23] George Meredith, "An Essay on Comedy," in Sypher, p. 33.
[24] Butcher, p. 375.

The comic style is characterized by incongruity and absurdity. Incongruity results whenever there is a discrepancy between what ought to be and what is, or between appearances and realities; absurdity results whenever logic is flagrantly violated, or whenever persons, situations, or ideas depart markedly from an anticipated or established norm. Whenever human beings are confronted with the incongruous or the absurd their usual response is laughter, a physiological response to the embarrassment that incongruity and absurdity provoke. The ability to laugh distinguishes men from beasts. Laughter is not absolutely necessary to comedy, however, as weeping is not absolutely necessary to tragedy. Often, the comic experience is effectively communicated whenever one intellectually perceives incongruity and absurdity, and with this perception (which need not result in laughter) comes the cathartic effect of comedy.

The incongruity and absurdity that characterize comedy are akin to the pity and terror that characterize tragedy in the same way that laughter and weeping are akin. Lord Byron in a famous line makes this point clear: "And if I laugh at any mortal thing 'Tis that I may not weep." This point is dramatized most effectively in "My Kinsman, Major Molineux." Robin, upon beholding his uncle on a rail, bursts into maniacal laughter. In reality his reaction is indistinguishable from either laughter or weeping. It is a physiological release from the overwhelming effects of incongruity, absurdity, pity, and terror which he experiences all at once in a blinding flash. In short, he is experiencing comedy and tragedy simultaneously. He "laughs only because he can suffer excruciatingly."[25] He must laugh because "Laughter is the result of an expectation which, of a sudden, ends in nothing."[26]

Of all the works being considered here, *The Adventures of Huckleberry Finn* best exemplifies comedy, and much of the comedy in Twain's novel can be interpreted most clearly in the light of specific statements by Bergson on the nature of comedy. The teacher would be well advised to consider the pedagogical usefulness of these statements, and to apply them accordingly. One must ever bear in mind, however, that the comedy in *The Adventures of Huckleberry Finn* is uneven in quality; that is, it is generally agreed that in the Phelps Farm incidents the aesthetic

[25] Sypher, p. 204.
[26] Kant, quoted by Bergson, p. 116.

quality of the comedy degenerates markedly. Yet some critics (of whom, more later) would disagree with this contention.

Bergson's main point is that comedy is impossible without the absurdity and incongruity which stem from human rigidity and inflexibility, and as a corollary to this point he adds that only laughter can redress this defect: "The rigid, the ready made, the mechanical in contrast with the supple, the everchanging and living . . . automatism in contrast with free activity, such are the defects that laughter singles out and would fain correct."[27] This notion is reminiscent of Dewey's that things in flux are vital, while those things that are static are stagnant. Bergson is really arguing here that the inner-directed man is not a fit subject for comedy because he is capable of effecting a meaningful experiential development. He is dynamic. His counterpart, the other-directed man, the tradition-directed man, the flat character, or naturalistic man is not. He is static. The latter type of man is less a person than the former. He is, in fact, more like a "thing," and "we laugh every time a person gives us the impression of being a thing."[28] We think immediately of Pap Finn or the Duke and the Dauphin whose failures as persons qualify them as comic subjects. Each qualifies, too, in that "a comic character is generally comic in proportion to his ignorance of himself."[29]

To Bergson the function of laughter is to intimidate by humiliating. For "Laughter is, above all, a corrective. Being intended to humiliate, it must make a painful impression on the person against whom it is directed. By laughter society avenges itself for the liberties taken with it."[30] The Duke and the Dauphin become the butts of laughter in this manner when the townsfolk, however cruelly, tar and feather them. The undertaker who conducts the funeral services for Peter Wilks is an uproariously comic character because he exemplifies "The attitudes, gestures, and movements of the human body [which] are laughable in exact proportion as that body reminds us of a mere machine. . . . This is no longer life; it is automatism established in life and imitating it."[31]

[27] Bergson, p. 145.
[28] *Ibid.*, p. 97.
[29] *Ibid.*, p. 71.
[30] *Ibid.*, p. 187.
[31] *Ibid.*, pp. 79, 81.

Often irony creates the materials of comedy. The disparity which exists between appearance and reality is often incongruous enough to shock one into laughter. For

A situation is invariably comic when it belongs simultaneously to two altogether independent series of events, and is capable of being interpreted in two entirely different meanings at the same time.[32]

This perhaps explains why one can find humor in Swift's "A Modest Proposal." The discrepancy between what is said and what is meant suggests an absurdity of the human condition that is at complete odds with a conventional morality; the discrepancy between Swift's content and style (a grave theme understated) does likewise. In *Billy Budd* the newspaper account of Billy's situation aboard *The Indomitable* is so at variance with reality as to border on the ludicrous, despite the true tragedy of the situation.

Often, an ironic misproportion between cause and effect or preparation and outcome can be comic. One thinks, for example, of the elaborate games played by Tom Sawyer and company, and the carefully worked out schemes of the Duke and the Dauphin which abort, and the resolution of Pap's to reform.

There is a type of humor, however, which suggests that man is basically sadistic. This, of course, is "sick" humor. It arises from the fact that

The passion of laughter is nothing else but a sudden glory, arising from a sudden conception of some eminency in ourselves, by comparison of the infirmity of others or with our own formerly.[33]

Mark Twain employs it in his presentation of Emmaline Grangerford and Harelip, one of the Wilks girls. The modern teenager is aware of it through the many "sick" jokes that have become part of present-day idiom. Yet Hobbes' statement need not be restricted to sick humor. In experiencing both tragedy and comedy, few of us can resist the temptation to take delight (albeit unconscious) from the fact that we are more fortunate than others. In this sense the cathartic effects of tragedy and comedy afford us security. We can endure the sufferings and humiliations of the hero-victims at a vicarious level by willingly suspending our sense of disbelief and pretending that the experience is real,

[32] *Ibid.*, p. 123.
[33] Thomas Hobbes, in Butcher, p. 374.

and that we are really they, though we know we are not.

Like tragedy, comedy can contribute to the full development of one's liberal education:

Comedy teaches us to look at life exactly as it is, undulled by scientific theories. Comedy banishes monstrous monotonousness. It teaches us to be responsive, to be honest, to interrogate ourselves and correct our pretentiousness. . . . The comic spirit is the ultimate civilizer in a dull, insensitive world.[34]

Comedy is a great democratizer. It humbles the proud and exalts the lowly. It helps to relieve us of the confusion that results from the baffling irreconcilables of experience. It is "a momentary and publicly useful resistance to authority and an escape from its pressures,"[35] as Huck Finn so well illustrates.

Comedy can correct incongruity and absurdity by chastisement. This is the job of satire which sets out to ridicule and poke fun at human stupidity and obtuseness for which human beings themselves are responsible. For "Whenever we are self-deceived, overblown, blinded by our pedantries, we deserve the scourge of the satirist. . . ."[36] However, the satirist does not ridicule those who are not to blame for their misfortune, unless he employs "sick" humor. One can find much of the satirist in Mark Twain. He holds up for good-natured ridicule all of those characters who are deserving of contempt, and in doing so reveals some sympathy for them. Jonathan Swift's satire, on the other hand is not good-natured. It is bitter and misanthropic, often not to be laughed at. Mark Twain's satirical thrusts in "The Man Who Corrupted Hadleyburg" and "The Mysterious Stranger" approach the Swiftian style, though they do not attain the artistic excellence of Swift's works.

Edward P. J. Corbett in commenting upon *The Catcher in the Rye* notes that "One of the most startling paradoxes about this book is that although it is immensely funny, there is not an ounce of humor in Holden himself."[37] Holden's lack of a sense of humor is what most markedly distinguishes him from Huck Finn, and contributes to his inability to adapt to the demands of his environment. Holden perceives

[34] Sypher, p. x.

[35] *Ibid.*, pp. 241–42.

[36] *Ibid.*, p. xiv.

[37] Edward P. J. Corbett, "Raise High the Barriers, Censors," *America*, 104 (January 7, 1961), p. 443.

the incongruous and the absurd all about him, but cannot apply the barb of laughter to these departures from the desired norm. As a natural Platonist he cannot tolerate or endure imperfection, inconsistency, or contradiction. He is not one of those who, like Huck Finn, can derive some therapy from comedy as suggested by Sypher: "Comedy can be a means of mastering our disillusions when we are caught in a dishonest or stupid society . . . [through a] wise laughter that brings a catharisis of our discontent."[38] Holdens inability to experience catharsis is what causes him to escape into a world of fantasy and to suffer his subsequent psychic collapse. It is significant that many of the youthful heroes who suffer misfortune and disaster are lacking in a sense of humor: Studs Lonigan, Martin Eden, Clyde Griffiths, and Willa Cather's Paul. This statement, of course, must be qualified by the fact that the more noble characters like Ike McCaslin and Sarty Snopes are lacking in a sense of humor also.

Like content and style, tragedy and comedy do not fit into neat, mutually exclusive categories. The two concepts serve as convenient cover terms between which there are overlappings, and within which there are sub-classes or variations. The main principles of tragedy have been laid out in the beginning of this chapter, and it has been suggested that a work like *Billy Budd* best exemplifies the tragic spirit, as against the pathetic spirit exemplified by such works as *Studs Lonigan* and *Death of a Salesman*. The pathetic spirit is a debased form of the tragic spirit by virtue of its naturalism, or by virtue of its melodramatic elements. In melodrama the writer relies heavily on situational suspense, the manipulation of the reader's emotions, oversimplification of theme, and improbable irony to achieve his "tragic" effects. Melodrama is unsophisticated tragedy. It is more understandable and accessible than true tragedy, but much less rewarding intellectually. It seldom involves its readers with profound, baffling questions which urgently demand answers and, even if it does, it resolves these questions through either a happy ending or an ambiguous ending which the reader has the option to make "happy" in his own mind. A work like *Uncle Tom's Cabin* represents melodrama at its worst; the trial scenes in *An American Tragedy* represent it at its best.

A work like *The Adventures of Huckleberry Finn* best exemplifies the comic spirit. But, as tragedy is debased by melodrama, so, too, is comedy

[38] Sypher, p. 245.

debased by farce, which is best represented by the Phelps Farm incidents in Twain's work. In farce the writer ovedroes his treatment of the
incongruous and the absurd by setting up ludicrously improbable
situations which many critics find intellectually offensive; the writer
employs every device at his command to force laughter in the same
manner that the melodramatic writer forces emotional responses. The
slapstick of The Three Stooges represents farce at its worst. Shakespeare's *Comedy of Errors* represents it at its best.

Nevertheless, though melodrama and farce are aesthetically inferior to tragedy and comedy they serve useful purposes in other respects.
First, they are valuable from a pedagogical standpoint. By comparing
and contrasting them with superior forms, the student learns how to
sharpen his value judgments. Exposure to the inferior helps one to appreciate better the superior. Most students respond negatively to the
latter part of *The Adventures of Huckleberry Finn.* Teachers can profitably
utilize this response in explaining the meaning of comedy. Second,
melodrama and farce can provide all of us a relief from the hard,
gruelling work that a proper study of tragedy and comedy entails.
They are valuable as "fun and relaxation" activities. Many students
welcome activities that can be enjoyed for their own sake, without
having to analyze them, and teachers would be wise to permit students
this indulgence. However, a steady diet of melodrama and farce can
be stultifying and unrewarding, and can lead to a complete breakdown
of taste. Finally, for those people who are intellectually limited or aca-
demically disinclined, the experience afforded by melodrama and
farce is more valuable than no aesthetic experience at all, and they can
provide pleasure and enjoyment for these students in a way that true
tragedy and comedy probably cannot.

The terms tragedy and comedy do not always apply easily to some
works. *Billy Budd* and *The Adventures of Huckleberry Finn* are notable
exceptions. Works like *The Red Badge of Courage* and *The Catcher in the Rye*
are not so easily classified. In a sense, *The Red Badge of Courage* is a
comedy in that Henry triumphs over fate completely. Yet there is no
humor in the work, except, perhaps, for the atypical dialects of the
soldiers. Many incidents in the work are melodramatic. Jim Conklin's
death is pathetic, not tragic. Holden is more of a tragic character than,
say, Studs Lonigan, but he is still more pathetic than tragic. Perhaps
Mr. Antolini is the only true tragic character in the work. In any case,
these evaluations are hard to make out of context.

Structure as style

Structure may be simply defined as the manner in which the artist shapes the parts of his work and combines them into a final whole. It is to a fictional work what the term "architecture" is to a building—the style of design. An understanding of the structure of a work of art is necessary for a fuller understanding of the meaning of the art work, for its total meaning constitutes more than what results from the sum of all its parts. How it is put together adds yet another dimension to its meaning.

To illustrate the importance of structure as a key to meaning, the teacher might employ a technique used by structural linguists in their analysis of words and sentences. The structural linguists devise nonsense sentences which are almost completely devoid of lexical meaning, and then proceed to show how meaning can be derived independently from structural and positional clues. Consider, for example, the statement: Before glooking and hamwafling their shimmerfroes, the hoppertums sontaptily strammerblooked the croly shrotiffers. Despite the fact that this statement cannot be paraphrased intelligibly, it yet contains a great deal more meaning than the semantic import of its individual words indicates. We know that it is not a question because it does not have the formal marker "?" at the end, and it is not "structured" with a verb at the beginning. The structures of the individual words signify several different meanings: time (-ed, -ing); plurality (-s); manner (-ly); adjectival modification (-ly). The order in which the words occur is a structural element which distinguishes the doers of action from the receivers of action, and the modifiers of parts of speech from the parts of speech being modified. Indeed, this nonsense sentence has more meaning than a scrambled "sense" sentence because its structure is consistent with that of an acceptable English sentence. Compare the following statements: (1) The people happily paid taxes to the government in return for its services. (2) for happily taxes return its to people services The paid in government the. Students can structure these words so as to create several sentences which differ in total meaning. Thus, in even so simple an organism as a sentence does structure determine meaning, and as a function of style it provides the artist with a variety of alternatives through which he can control and develop his content.

Understanding structure involves an understanding of how a part of an art work justifies its existence as a contributor to the total effect of the work, much in the same manner that a member of an athletic team or a band or an army or a choir is essential to the total success of the group acting as a unit. Structure is what has "become" as a result of a series of subsidiary, interrelated "becomings," each an independent but necessary element. It is the apples, pears, plums, and other fruits that add up to the comprehensive concept "fruit"; it is the gestalt that gives definition to the atomistic elements of which it is composed; it crystallizes into a comprehensible entity, a series of disparate, often disconnected, lesser entities; it is "The rule . . . of necessity . . . the inner law which secures cohesion of the parts."[1]

The student may gain an understanding of the structure of an art form either deductively or inductively. If he does so deductively, he will comprehend the total effect without being consciously aware of the parts that contribute to it; if he does so inductively, he will comprehend the total effect by reconstructing its parts and fitting them together much in the manner that one works a jigsaw puzzle. George Winchester Stone points out: "Every literary work has its design: its theme is worked out in a certain apprehensible way, manifest in the total structure and in the finest details of execution. A perception of organic form should certainly be expected of students of literature."[2] This "perception of organic form" is the essence of interpreting structure. Ordinarily, it is wise to employ both the deductive and inductive approaches in combination in having students interpret structure.

The study of structure fulfills a basic human need. Guth observes: "We have an elementary need for organizing the flux of multifarious impressions in such a way as to make possible meaningful response. We have an elementary need for order: for structuring experience so as to

---

[1] Butcher, p. 166.
[2] Stone, pp. 58–59.

make it intelligible and manageable."[3] What the student learns to do with art, we hope, can have transfer value in his encounters with the realities of life. He should learn "something essential about how writing not merely records but organizes experience. He sees how mere sequence is transformed into structure. He sees how the essential is distinguished from the peripheral, the meaningful from the trivial."[4] In short, he acquires the substance of a sound liberal education. For art at its best "creates an idea of order where, to the inartistic or unphilosophical observer, life is only a whirl of action and a chaos of emotion. . . . The crude matter of life assumes significance from the shaping hand of the artist."[5] It is Holden Caulfield's misfortune (perhaps tragedy) that despite his artistic and philosophical sensitivity he is unable to make a fine art of living, to order and structure his experience sensibly and productively. Unlike Huck Finn, he must settle for "a whirl of action and a chaos of emotion."

A work of art may be structured according to a classical design or a romantic design. To Cox, "The Classic Spirit is the disinterested search for perfection; it is the love of clearness and reasonableness and self-control. It seeks to express disciplined emotion. . . . It strives for the essential rather than the accidental, the eternal rather than the momentary."[6] Hamm expands on this conception: "The virtues of classicism . . . are the structural virtues of clarity, simplicity, and grace."[7] The romantic design, on the other hand, is characterized differently. It is not so disciplined, develops spontaneously rather than according to a predetermined pattern or immutable laws, gives freer rein to the artist's individuality, and is given more to uniqueness, unconventionality, and improvisation. All this is not to say, however, that either one of these types of design is intrinsically superior to the other. In the hands of a gifted artist either can attain aesthetic superiority.

Perhaps one of the best ways to illustrate to students the distinguishing features of the classical and romantic structures can be found in the comparisons and contrasts that one could make between the various art forms. Alexander Pope's "Essay on Criticism" best exemplifies the

[3] Guth, p. 248.

[4] *Ibid.*, p. 176.

[5] Gassner, p. xli.

[6] Kenyon Cox, *The Classic Point of View* (New York: Scribner, 1911), p. 3.

[7] Victor M. Hamm, *The Pattern of Criticism* (Milwaukee: Bruce, 1951), p. 65.

manner and matter of the classical structure in literature. His rhymed couplets are carefully polished, balanced statements whose content is controlled, restrained, and rational. In this essay Pope argues that the best art is patterned on the classical ideals of symmetry, proportion, and moderation. In contrast to Pope is Walt Whitman, whose "Song of Myself" best exemplifies the manner and matter of the romantic structure. Whitman employs the unrhymed and arhythmical patterns of free verse. His statements are unrestrained and immoderate, a "barbaric yawp." He often exalts the sensual and the emotional over the rational and the spiritual, and uses his poetry as a sounding board for the expression of his ego.[8]

In art forms other than literature the classical and romantic structures are observable. A Greek temple is decidedly a classical structure; a Gothic cathedral or medieval castle, romantic. A Rembrandt painting is for the most part a classical structure; modern abstract or impressionistic art, romantic. A Mozart or Haydn symphony is classical; a Wagnerian opera, romantic. Classical principles inhere in consistent geometric figures like the square or the circle; the romantic in parabolic or elongated figures. A man-made structure like a clock illustrates classical principles; a natural structure like a tree illustrates romantic principles.

Perhaps the best way to comprehend the structure of a fictional work is through an examination of its plot. Very simply, "Plot is the sequence of incidents or events of which a story is composed."[9] "It is a narrative of events arranged in their time sequence."[10] It is the action that "forms a complete whole: it is a coherent series of events, standing in organic relation to one another and bound together by the law of cause and effect. The internal centre, the pivot upon which the whole system turns, is the plot."[11]

Plot *per se* "is the lowest and simplest of literary organisms."[12] At its lowest level it simply tells what happens in a story. And "Because

[8] Disclaimers are in order here. These statements certainly do not apply to all the poetry of Pope or Whitman.

[9] Perrine, *Story and Structure*, p. 61.

[10] Forster, p. 27.

[11] Butcher, p. 349.

[12] Forster, pp. 27–28.

plot is [usually] the easiest element in fiction to comprehend and put into words, the beginning reader tends to equate it with the content of the work."13 Unfortunately, this equation occurs much too often in the book reports typically offered in the secondary school. At the elementary school level, one can often be quite satisfied if the student can extract the main outlines of action from a fictional work. At the secondary level, however, an understanding simply of what happens is not enough. One would hope that the student could interpret the significance of what happens. Plot summary serves admirably as a starting point for literary analysis. But, it is no substitute for critical interpretation.

All this is not to say, however, that plot is necessarily an inferior "literary organism." For despite its admittedly simplistic nature. "it is [paradoxically] the highest common factor to all the complicated organisms known as novels."14 Plot may be compared to a length of thread which by itself is of little value. When, however, it is used to hold together a complicated tapestry it assumes a form and function of great value. So, too, with plot. In and of itself it is but a mere shadow of the fictional work. As themes, characters, and symbols attach to it, however it becomes an integral and necessary part of the work. Even so, plot by itself can be very complicated. One thinks of multiple-plot works like James Joyce's *Ulysses* and Faulkner's *The Sound and the Fury* and *As I Lay Dying* in which involved time relationships and subtle twists of action make of plot a staggeringly complex organism indeed. But these works are not ordinarily high school fare, and thus need not concern the teacher as far as his typical teaching assignments are concerned. However, it is desirable for teachers to study these types of fiction so as to be qualified to teach the more conventional works effectively and meaningfully.

The nomenclature of drama is useful for presenting to students the concept of plot development, since most fictional works are in a sense modified plays. On the blackboard the teacher may construct a horizontal time line which can represent the beginning, middle, and ending of the work in question. As one reads into a work, time passes and things begin to happen (action) which can be plotted on a vertical scale. The vertical element can represent exposition, in which the

13 Perrine, *Story and Structure*, p. 61.
14 Forster, p. 28.

author presents a background; rising action, in which complications ensue; foreshadowings, in which future situations are hinted at; reversals, due to digression or unexpected situational changes; climax, the point of highest interest or concern in which two forces are at loggerheads; falling action, in which interest flags because the opposing forces have spent their energies; and resolution, in which the problems posed in the work are partially or completely solved. Many other things may be noted as this time-action graph is plotted: parallel subplots; authorial shifts of tone, attitude, point of view, and locale; flashbacks; comic relief; rate of development of character and theme; and the author's sense of proportion in his treatment of various scenes. There are few pedagogical devices which lend themselves so readily to the inductive approach to teaching as this one. Teachers can easily draw out of the students all the pertinent details necessary to construct such a graph, and after it is constructed it provides insight into the total structure or gestalt of the work.

Point of view is the element of structure which defines the perspective from which a story is told, and helps to determine the manner in which the plot is unfolded for the reader. In choosing the point of view he wishes to employ, the author, in effect, makes a contractual agreement with the reader, and is obliged either to maintain a consistent point of view or to give fair warning should he decide to change it, in order not to confuse the reader. Some authors, like Faulkner in *As I Lay Dying*, take extreme liberties in shifting their points of view, and thus burden their readers to a point where their works "cannot be read; they must be studied"[15] to be appreciated. In effect these authors take an extremely romantic attitude of art for art's sake rather than for purposes of communication. They write for themselves, not for their readers. Faulkner sounds this attitude in his statement, "Let the reader be damned."[16]

The author has, essentially, three alternatives with respect to choice of point of view: the first person, the third person, and the dramatic points of view. The first- and third-person points of view have various advantages and disadvantages which the author must take into account in structuring his work. The dramatic point of view is distinct from the other two in a manner which will be considered shortly.

[15] Booth, p. 325.
[16] *Ibid.*, p. 89.

In first-person narration, one of the major characters[17] of the work speaks directly to the audience, and he refers to himself as "I." There is a distinct advantage in employing the first-person technique. The reader gets an eyewitness, first-hand account of the situation of the story from an active participant, and thus becomes more immediately involved in the action. This involvement occurs in reading *The Adventures of Huckleberry Finn*. The perceptive, sensitive reader engages in a kind of silent conversation with Huck, who establishes personal contact immediately through his disarming, chatty manner. However, the first-person technique has disadvantages in that if the narrator is unreliable or prejudiced there is the danger that he may distort the facts, as Holden does to some extent. It is interesting that in *The Catcher in the Rye* Holden's view of things predominates. He reports the actions and conversations of others, which he interprets in the light of his own distorted experiences. If Ackley or Antolini were to tell the story one would get an entirely different view of things. Nevertheless, Salinger is artist enough to present Holden in such a way that the real truth of the matter often filters through to the reader. The reader has to earn this insight, however, through a concentrated reading of the text.

In third-person narration, the speaker is a detached observer, not a participating character. The advantage of this technique lies in the speaker's not being directly involved in the action, and thus being more capable of objectivity. But this is not always the case. The author may use the third person to pretend detachment, while in actuality he propagandizes a particular bias by literally putting carefully chosen words into the mouths of his characters. Harriet Beecher Stowe and George Eliot are notorious in this regard. There is another advantage in that the third person can more naturally be in command of a fuller knowledge of the problems and situations of the story, and can literally read the thoughts and emotions of the characters. It would be utterly out of place for a first-person narrator to enjoy this privilege. He would become ludicrously superhuman, and would reduce the story to a fantasy. Even so, the omniscience of the third-person narrator must often be kept within bounds. Otherwise, he, too, may become something of a deity.

The dramatic point of view differs from that of first and third person in that it approaches more nearly the conditions of a play pre-

---

[17] At times he may be a minor character as some critics believe Ishmael to be.

sented on the stage. That is, there is no intermediary narrator between the reader and the work. The personal voice of the narrator is stilled. Nobody reports the scene; rather, it appears. The experience speaks for itself, and the reader partakes of it more fully without the assistance of a go-between.[18] The dramatic point of view can be best demonstrated to students through a study of such plays as Thornton Wilder's *Our Town* and Tennessee Williams' *The Glass Menagerie* in which narrators intrude and present commentary. When the narrators are silent, the characters speak for themselves and the dramatic point of view is maintained.

Modern writers of fiction like Joyce and Faulkner have labored diligently to efface themselves as narrators of their works. Booth points out:

Since Flaubert, many authors and critics have been convinced that 'objective' or 'impersonal' or 'dramatic' modes of narration are naturally superior to any mode that allows for direct appearances by the author or his reliable spokesman. . . . This shift has been reduced to a convenient distinction between 'showing' which is artistic, and 'telling' which is inartistic.[19]

However, it seems that the "show-tell" distinction is artificial. For an author may show through telling and tell through showing without in any way impairing the aesthetic merit of his work. It is virtually impossible to efface the author completely: "The author's voice is never really silenced. It is, in fact, one of the things we read fiction for, and we are never troubled by it unless the author makes a great to-do about his own superior naturalness."[20] Indeed, authors reveal themselves even in the titles they assign to their works. "The Waste Land?" "Who says so?" Booth asks.[21]

The fact is that all good fiction unfolds itself in such a way that, regardless of whether the author chooses first- or third-person presentation (and he must choose one or the other unless he is writing a play), the reader engages in an intense dramatic experience. When Colonel Sherburn makes his vitriolic speech to the townsfolk, the reader is scarcely aware that Huck Finn is reporting his words and that Mark

---

[18] Percy Lubbock, *The Craft of Fiction* (New York: Scribner, 1929), in Aldridge, pp. 10, 11, 14.
[19] Booth, p. 8.
[20] *Ibid.*, p. 60.
[21] *Ibid.*, p. 101.

Twain is telling Huck what to say. No one thinks the less of *Moby Dick* because every word in it is uttered by Ishmael. Yet, Ishmael is so completely removed from the narrative at times that in the stateroom scene in which Ahab and Starbuck call a showdown, the reader feels that he is watching a pure stage performance. Melville's expanded intrusions in *Billy Budd* in no way detract from the merit of that work, and Willa Cather is not to be discredited as an artist because she "tells" rather than "shows" in "Paul's Case," a work whose 8500 words include only sixty words of actual dialogue. To be sure, authorial intrusion can be offensive, as in *Uncle Tom's Cabin*. It need not be so, however, in the hands of a talented artist.

Through the so-called stream-of-consciousness technique the dramatic point of view is often achieved. This technique differs from that of the conventional soliloquy and the interior monologue which are both structured as logical arguments, the former being presented directly to an audience as a conversation with no feedback, the latter as a conversation with oneself in the presence of a tuned-in audience. In stream-of-consciousness—or perhaps it ought more properly to be called stream-of-unconsciousness—there is no argumentative structure, no predetermined pattern of presentation, and no conscious intention on the part of the character to narrate directly to an audience. The audience, instead, overhears the thought processes of the character like a psychiatrist psychoanalyzing a patient who is spontaneously voicing whatever may be in his mind at the moment. Often, but not necessarily always, what is presented by the character resembles a dream sequence, a series of fragmented, half-formed thoughts and images which do not yield readily to sensible interpretation. This free-association, free-wheeling method of presentation is best exemplified by Nick Adams, who in his American uniform is commissioned to bolster the morale of the Italian troops at the front: "And there was Gaby Delys oddly enough with feathers on, with feather off, the great Gaby, and my name's Harry Pilcer, too. . . . and he could see that hill every night when he dreamed with Sacre Coeur, blown white like a soap bubble."[22] The burden now is on the reader to make sense of this statement. He cannot rely on authorial help as in a soliloquy or an interior monologue. In this respect he truly becomes a co-creator of the work, but he does so at the cost of the added labor required for interpretation. Ordinarily, the

[22] Ernest Hemingway, "A Way You'll Never Be," *The Snows of Kilimanjaro and Other Stories* (New York: Scribner, 1961), p. 88.

abor is too much for the common reader, and it thus becomes the job of he professional critic to make the work accessible to him.

The structure of *The Adventures of Huckleberry Finn* has engendered much controversy among critics. The novel begins in farce and ends n farce, and the two sections of farce, which constitute roughly forty percent of the work, provide a framework for the middle section, which many critics seem to consider high-level fictional art. The question at ssue resolves itself into whether the farce detracts from the total value of the work, or gives added substance to its total effect—in short, whether the farce is a negative or positive aesthetic force.

Joseph Wood Krutch has said that *The Adventures of Huckleberry Finn* is a bad novel but a great book: "Much of it is so improbable as to become at times wholly unconvincing on one level of understanding. It is also episodic, clumsily plotted, and sometimes as crudely melodramatic as a dime novel."[23] Despite this aesthetic failing, however, Krutch concedes that the novel is an accomplished epic on the evils of slavery.

Leo Marx, in an involved argument, contends that the most serious motive in the work—the freeing of Jim is denigrated through the introduction of Tom Sawyer, who serves to reduce Jim to a servile, fawning minstrel and Huck to a comic pawn.[24] Marx, it seems, takes the farcical elements of the novel much too seriously. He is probably the most outspoken criticizer of Twain's structural shift.

Other critics are less severe on Twain. R. P. Adams, though aware of Twain's failure to maintain unity of plot, praises the work on the grounds that

Its unity and coherence are thematic and symbolic—imaginative in the Coleridgian sense. Its elements are not related by the logic of cause and effect. Instead, they are fused in any organization of imagery that transcends any concept of plot or story line as a series of casually related events.[25]

To substantiate his contention that theme and symbol take precedence over plot consistency as effective devices of unity and coherence, Adams argues that the farcical elements of the novel serve the valuable function of satirizing the sentimental literature and conventional genteelness of

[23] Krutch, "Speaking of Books," *New York Times Book Review*, May 23, 1954, p. 2.
[24] Leo Marx, "Mr. Eliot, Mr. Trilling, and *Huckleberry Finn*," in Bradley, *Huck Finn*, p. 328–41.
[25] R. P. Adams, "The Unity and Coherence of *Huckleberry Finn*," in Bradley, *Huck Finn*, p. 343.

the times, as well as the quixotic stupidity of Tom Sawyer.[26] Lionel Trilling sees aesthetic merit in the farce ending as a device "to permit Huck to return to his anonymity, to give up the role of hero, to fall into the background which he prefers. . . . For this purpose nothing could serve better than the mind of Tom Sawyer with its literary furnishings."[27] And, arguing substantially the same point, T. S. Eliot states that Huck, unlike Tom, "has no beginning and end. Hence, he can only disappear; and his disappearance can only be accomplished by bringing forward another performer to obscure the disappearance in a cloud of whimsicalities."[28]

Robert L. Vales offers an interesting argument regarding the necessity of the farcical elements as contributors to the total structure and meaning of the novel. Throughout the novel there occurs a thief-theft pattern which culminates in the final stealing of Jim. In the early parts the boys play at robbery. Pap steals Huck and in turn sees society robbing him of $6000. Huck escapes from Pap through theft. Thievery versus borrowing is a subject of casuistic discussion for Huck. The robbers on the *Walter Scott* indulge in thievery and are in turn robbed of their freedom. Harvey steals Sophia. The Dauphin steals $87.75 from the townsfolk and the bag of gold. He in turn is robbed of his loot. The Duke steals Jim and sells him for forty dollars. Vales maintains that this series of minor thefts lead up to the grand theft—the stealing of Jim, and that the farcical conditions under which he is stolen are consistent with the ludicrous (tragic?) irony that he ought never to have been put in this position from the beginning. In this sense, then, the shift into slapstick is justified because it highlights ironic truth effectively.[29]

From a pedagogical standpoint it is really irrelevant whether or not the book has an irredeemable flaw in its overall structure. The fact that this point is controversial and can be argued with equal force regardless of the stance that one takes makes the novel highly teachable, and provides material for endless discussion. Even more importantly, however, it provides students with an occasion to formulate and develop an original insight of their own—the ultimate achievement in the process of education.

[26] *Ibid.*, p. 355.
[27] Lionel Trilling, "The Greatness of *Huck Finn*," in Bradley, *Huck Finn*, p. 318.
[28] T. S. Eliot, "Introduction to *Huck Finn*," in Bradley, *Huck Finn*, p. 327.
[29] Robert L. Vales, "Thief and Theft in *Huckleberry Finn*," *American Literature*, XXXVII (January, 1966), pp. 420–29.

A certain unity of structure is maintained in *The Adventures of Huckleberry Finn* through the recurrent symbol of the Mississippi River in the same manner that the material universe does so in *The Red Badge of Courage*: "The most striking thing in *The Red Badge* is the peculiar equation constantly maintained by its imagery. Anything pertaining to war in this book of war is apt to be visualized in terms of the material universe, and this universe itself is constantly personified."[30] As the Mississippi River and its related imagery provide a context or framework for the drama of *Huck Finn*, so, too, does the natural universe in *The Red Badge of Courage*, the fomer signifying truth and calm in the midst of deception and confusion, the latter signifying the indifference of nature to the concerns of men fighting for survival.

The overall structure of *The Red Badge of Courage* is more unified than that of *The Adventures of Huckleberry Finn*. Crane's work adheres more to the classical principles of design than does Twain's. Many of the episodes in *The Adventures of Huckleberry Finn* do not effectively coalesce. For example, Chapter XXII, in which Sherburn makes his speech, also contains the incident in which the circus rider feigns drunkenness and gives the sadistic crowd a thrill. There seems little justification to juxtapose such unrelated, disparate episodes in one chapter. (Nevertheless, a perceptive student might very well discover some principle of consistency in this juxtaposition.) In *The Red Badge of Courage* all the incidents seem somehow to relate more logically to the total effect: Jim Conklin's death, John Wilson's fear for his personal safety, Henry's rationalizations, and many more.

In executing his work, Crane achieves a classical economy of effect. He indulges in no digressions, nor does he philosophize on history or the nature of war, as Tolstoy does in *War and Peace*. In fact, he never even mentions the American Civil War by name, though one can infer it as the setting through his descriptions of the uniforms and his use of the term "Reb." He develops his story both logically and chronologically, moving from the general to the specific (from the "youth" to Henry Fleming), and from a panoramic view to a particular scene (from the Army to the regiment to the platoon). One could argue perhaps that Henry's rationalizations are digressions which detract from the advancement of the main action. But it seems, rather, that they indirectly intensify the action by providing Henry with the proper provocation to act more forcefully at his next opportunity.

[30] John W. Schroeder, "Stephen Crane Embattled," in Bradley, *Red Badge*, p. 243.

As Vales sees a thief-theft pattern in *The Adventures of Huckleberry Finn* which serves to unify its structure, Stallman sees a despair-hope pattern in *The Red Badge of Courage* which does likewise, and Henry's mind provides the stage on which the drama of this pattern is enacted.[31] Students could be asked to examine the validity of this contention as they read the work. Walcutt sees a structural pattern in *The Red Badge of Courage* which has unusual pedagogical possibilities. He likens Henry's situation to that of a squirrel caught in the enclosure of an equilateral triangle, scurrying from side to side in a panic, and sometimes getting stuck at the angle where two sides coincide. The sides represent in turn instinct, ideal, and circumstance.[32] Indeed this image truly epitomizes Henry's situation, and accurately portrays the overall structure of the work. It is a valid image which the student may employ as a guideline in tracing out the manner in which the work is developed.

As a triangle may be used as a graphic device to explain the structure of *The Red Badge of Courage*, so may a square be used to explain the structure of *Billy Budd*. Every statement in the work attempts in some way to answer four basic questions which may be represented by the four sides of a square: Who is Billy Budd? What happens to him? Why does it happen? What are the consequences of its happening? Through these questions one can see the main outlines of the plot of the story, and to give substance to this plot Melville employs a series of digressions which provide the reader with an expanded exposition, and raise subtler, more difficult questions. These digressions take many forms, and Melville inserts them directly in his role as third-person, omniscient narrator in complete command of his material. He discusses the historical background of the French Revolution and its present-day relevance; makes many allusions to pertinent Biblical motifs; discusses at length the mutiny problem in the British Navy; introduces Lord Nelson as a foil to Captain Vere; has the purser and surgeon engage in a dialogue which highlights the dichotomy that exists between empirical knowledge and intuitive knowledge; and many others. Melville does not moralize in this process. Rather, he transforms the four basic questions, which are comparatively easy to answer, into a very difficult question: How does one reconcile the mutually antagonistic

[31] Stallman, "Notes Toward an Analysis of *Red Badge*, in Bradley, *Red Badge*, pp. 249–50.
[32] Charles C. Walcutt, "American Literary Naturalism: A Divided Stream," in Bradley, *Red Badge*, p. 280.

demands of military, natural, and divine law? This is one, but by no means the only, approach that the teacher may employ in assisting students to comprehend the basic structure of the work.

Despite the fact that *The Catcher in the Rye* is narrated in a seemingly rambling, stream-of-consciousness manner by Holden Caulfield, it yet has a unity of structure by virtue of Holden's consistency of character, and the sustained emotional tone of the work. Often, Holden seems to be talking in a perfunctory manner, but a careful examination of his statements reveals that every word is crucial to his entire statement, and that all his statements literally teem with essential information and overflow in a surge of connotations. To illustrate this, students might be asked to read just the first two pages of the work, and then to list all the things that are either expressed or implied by Holden's words. The final outcome of this exploration often proves nothing short of astounding to the student. For what seems on the surface to be careless small talk is in reality a carefully structured complex of facts and ideas.

Winesburg, Ohio presents some interesting problems with respect to structure. There is a unity in the work in that Anderson welds all its parts together through the main character, George Willard, who appears in almost all the incidents; in the fact that Anderson maintains unity of place, since all the characters are either from Winesburg or their fortunes are determined there; and in the fact that he maintains a consistent existential tone throughout, except for the epiphanic "Awakening" that George and Mary White experience. Nevertheless, the parts of the work do not cohere as do the parts in, say, *Billy Budd* or *The Red Badge of Courage* or *The Catcher in the Rye.* Anderson seems unable to develop one character or incident in depth. Instead he spreads out his artistic energies over many characters and situations. His most sustained treatment occurs in his account of the Jesse Bentley dynasty. Even here, however, he incorporates extraneous elements as padding, and he fills but forty pages. In this sense, *Winesburg, Ohio* is more an anthology of short stories, loosely connected, than a tightly structured novel. It is to Anderson's credit, however, that the separate units of the novel maintain a high-level structural unity within themselves, if not always in relation to each other.

Frederick J. Hoffman sees a tripartite structure in *An American Tragedy:* "Description of Cause," "Act," and "Reconsideration of

Cause."[33] This analysis certainly squares with the facts of the work, and can serve as a starting point for a more detailed analysis. The same structure is apparent in Knowles' *A Separate Peace*. With respect to "Act," however, an interesting contrast develops, which can be best interpreted in the light of Aristotle's dictum that the artist "should prefer probable impossibilities to improbable possibilities"[34] in constructing his fictional situations. This is a passage that is difficult to interpret. What Aristotle probably means by it is that freak twists of fate ought not to be crucial in affecting a course of significant events. As in true tragedy, human intentions and volition ought to have some play, too, in controlling destiny. Dreiser violates Aristotle's guideline at the climactic moment in the boat when Clyde Griffiths seems to suffer a paralysis of will. A highly improbable accident consummates his intention, and creates an uncomfortably fuzzy moral problem which the "Reconsideration of Cause" does not resolve, despite the involved and intricate arguments of both the defense and the prosecution. When Gene Forrester causes Finny's fall from the tree, however, we have definite proof that it was intended: "Holding firmly to the trunk, I took a step toward him, and then my knees bent and I jounced the limb."[35] Gene's situation differs from Clyde's, however, in that the former acts without deliberation, while the latter fails to act despite deliberation. In each case a moral dilemma presents itself. But Gene's situation is more probable because fate plays a small part in his actions. He becomes in effect a victim of his unconsciousness—which, of course, is conditioned by his consciousness but not determined by it. He is by nature constitutionally incapable of committing such an act deliberately, though he is capable of doing it spontaneously without benefit of reflection. In any case the situations of both boys raise an interesting semantic problem, which the teacher may use for purposes of discussion—the difference in meaning that exists between deliberation and intention with regard to the degree of personal responsibility one must incur for an act. These two terms may be used, for example, to define the difference between first-degree and second-degree murder.

When artists permit improbable possibilities in order to create special effects they are guilty of plot manipulation in much the same

[33] Frederick J. Hoffman, *The Modern Novel in America* (Chicago: Regnery, 1951), p. 48.

[34] Aristotle, p. 95.

[35] John Knowles, *A Separate Peace* (New York: Dell Publishing Co., 1965), p. 71.

manner as the deus ex machina of Greek drama. Often, this kind of manipulation puts an undue burden on the reader. Dreiser permits the highly improbable incident to occur on the boat because he is trying to create a moral problem which can be resolved only in naturalistic terms. In doing so, however, he does not touch upon the typical or the universal in human experience, and thus makes it harder for the reader to sympathize or identify with Clyde. As a result, if there is any true tragedy in this work it is not properly Clyde's.

Another form of plot manipulation occurs when the author indulges in the surprise ending in order to highlight an irony. The most flagrant example of this, of course, occurs in *The Adventures of Huckleberry Finn* when we learn that Jim has been free all along without knowing it. Perhaps this is the greatest weakness of the work. Faulkner does substantially the same thing in *Intruder in the Dust* by having the wrong man in the grave. In "My Kinsman, Major Molineux" Hawthorne handles his "surprise" more artistically. The reader is given many significant hints, farce is avoided, and more probability attaches to the situation. Even so, the way the townsfolk respond to Robin's request for information may be viewed by some as bordering on the improbable. Hawthorne's brilliant epiphany more than compensates for this failing, however.

Yet another form of plot manipulation occurs when the artist inserts suspense devices in order to capture and sustain reader interest. Truman Capote does this in *Other Voices, Other Rooms* by not making it possible for Joel to see his sick father, and by creating a mysterious woman who he never tells us is in reality the transvestite Cousin Randolph dressed as a woman. In *On the Road* Kerouac creates reader interest by his constant references to Dean Moriarty's colorful derelict father, who always seems just about ready to make an appearance, but never does.

A certain amount of plot manipulation is evident in some of the most accomplished works of fiction. One observes melodramatic flourishes even in Melville's treatment of Ahab. The artist has to be permitted this indulgence to a degree, especially the comic artist. It is necessary for the teacher and the student, however, to be able to distinguish between permissible plot manipulation and outright plot mismanagement. Perhaps Twain is most guilty of this aesthetic offense. One may observe it, too, in Fitzgerald's *This Side of Paradise*, in which

Amory Blaine changes from a flippant, carefree young man to a morbidly serious adult, abruptly and mechanically, without any warning
to the reader.

The concept of structure provides the teacher with a pedagogical
device which can prove of substantial value in the teaching of content.
The distinguished scientist-psychologist Jerome Bruner, who has in
recent years directed his talents and energies to the problems of pedagogy speaks tellingly to this point:

The teaching and learning of structure, rather than simply the mastery of
facts and techniques, is at the center of the classic problem of transfer. . . . If
earlier learning is to render later learning easier, it must do so by providing a
general picture in terms of which the relations between things encountered
earlier and later are made as clear as possible.[36]

Bruner concludes his discussion most convincingly:

Knowledge one has acquired without sufficient structure to tie it together is
knowledge that is likely to be forgotten. . . . Organizing facts in terms of principles and ideas from which they may be inferred is the only known way of
reducing the quick rate of loss of human memory.[37]

[36] Jerome S. Bruner, *The Process of Education* (New York: Knopf, 1960), p. 12.
[37] *Ibid.*, pp. 31–32.

Conclusion

Teachers often experience great difficulty in trying to convince students that there are real values to be gained from a study of literature. It should be the aim of all teachers "to present literature so effectively that no question of its direct usefulness arises—so that it becomes for the student an interesting (and therefore pleasurable) experience in itself."[1] For through literature one can learn of the "Why" of living, and, ideally, "He who knows a Why of living surmounts almost every How."[2]

Burton observes correctly that "Few adolescents would admit openly to an interest in 'philosophy of life.' Yet teenagers are keenly concerned with values, with the things that people live for, and with the motives that impel men."[3] It is the function of literature, therefore, to take us "through imagination deeper into the real world. . . . It gives us a keener awareness of what it is to be a human being in a

[1] John S. Lewis and Jean C. Sisk, *Teaching English*, 7–12 (New York: American Book Co., 1963), p. 195.

[2] Nietzsche, in Loban, p. 601.

[3] Burton, p. 58.

universe sometimes friendly, sometimes hostile."[4] It "enables us to explore the recesses of man's head and heart with a torch."[5]

Loban sees in literature the means through which "we can achieve freedom from the penalties and restrictions of singularity. Suspending our own values we look at life through the eyes of [the artist],"[6] whose insights encompass the entire spectrum of human experience. George Winchester Stone sees in it the means through which the student

builds and refines his own system of values through the process of experiencing a multitude of choices vicariously—choices that his normal life, his so-called 'practical life' would not afford him. . . . Literature offers the living example of events and of characters in action.[7]

In this respect the study of literature can be of substantial value even in the so-called "life adjustment" curriculum, which has in recent years been under attack by liberal-arts oriented critics of American education. Literature cannot be taught in a vacuum. The pleasure which the reader derives from its study may have a pragmatic as well as an aesthetic component in its realization. Loban grants that "Helping readers relate literature to life is one responsibility of the teacher, but such interaction is possible only if the elements of the book actually touch elements in the reader's experience."[8] Many of the works under consideration in this discussion should serve as useful resources towards achieving this end.

In keeping with the spirit of a scientific age, modern critics have attempted to interpret literature clinically and objectively in the manner of a research scientist analyzing a phenomenon of nature. To a degree this approach has much to commend it. It encourages the student to examine a work carefully and to avoid hasty judgments of the work's worth. It discourages prejudgment and fuzzy subjectivism.[9]

[4] Perrine, *Story and Structure*, p. 4.

[5] David Daiches, *A Study of Literature for Readers and Critics* (Ithaca: Cornell University Press, 1948), p. 24.

[6] Loban, p. 277.

[7] Stone, p. 177.

[8] Loban, p. 279.

[9] Even so, one can find many examples of subjectivism in the critical statements of some of the leading exponents of the New Criticism, such as John Crowe Ransom and Robert Penn Warren.

This approach works only to a point, however. All great art has elusive qualities which do not yield completely to clinical examination in much the same manner that religious truths do not yield completely to the methods of logic and reason. An element of intuition or faith is necessary to complete one's sense of understanding of either art or religion.

In order to have critical validity, the subjective or impressionistic approach to literary interpretation requires the full use of one's faculties of imagination, "a mental activity which—because it is relatively free from realistic demands—enables one to summon up images, feelings, memories, sensations, intuitions."[10] Loban feels that the New Critics have perhaps gone too far in their clinicism:

Too heavy an emphasis upon logical thought—to the exclusion of imagination and inspiration—eliminates the zest and satisfaction of learning. . . . Imagination, reverie, and intuition, all these forms of mental activity nourished by man's internal needs and impulses. Thinking shifts rapidly back and forth along the scale, never completely realistic, never completely imaginative. The mature individual maintains a delicate balance, emphasizing according to the situation the requirements of outer reality or the inner needs of his personality.[11]

And, counselling a more moderate and balanced approach to literary interpretation, he states:

For fostering imaginative thinking the English teacher's best resource is literature. Using both rational and imaginative thought, both referential and emotive language, literature requires alertness from a wide range of human response. Properly appreciated, literature requires a reader to be wide awake. . . . It promotes in him an equilibrium between reason and feeling, a harmony that diminishes the petty, narrow concerns always ready to consume his life, replacing these with a refreshing, resonant awareness of being alive.[12]

These statements, though overly idealistic in spots, deserve close perusal by the teacher of English. Even many scientists see a great value in imaginative thinking in their particular disciplines. Jerome Bruner best expresses this point of view:

Intuitive thinking, the training of hunches, is a much neglected and essential feature of productive thinking not only in formal academic disciplines but also

[10] Loban, p. 118.
[11] *Ibid.*, p. 117.
[12] *Ibid.*, p. 130.

in everyday life. The shrewd guess, the fertile hypothesis, the courageous leap to a tentative conclusion—these are the most valuable coin of the thinker at work. . . . Can school children be led to master this gift?[13]

Emphatically, our students must "be led to master this gift."

Done properly, the job of literary interpretation is as hard as the job of literary creation. An accomplished work of art stands on its own merits in an absolute sense. In a relative sense, however, it has only as much value as the reader is able to draw from it, and what the reader draws from it is in direct proportion to the effort he is willing to apply to it. Even so, "There are no easy rules for literary judgment. Such judgment depends ultimately on our perceptivity, intelligence, and experience."[14] The artist can do only so much. He "is an interpreter, not an inventor. Like a good actor he is an intermediary between a segment of experience and an audience,"[15] which then reconstructs this experience in the light of its own insights and capacities. This creates certain difficulties for the teacher, however, because of the wide variations of insight and capacity that exist among students. For this reason the spiral curriculum has much to commend it. Through this approach, which moves from the simple to the complex in a circular ascent, the student may study a work like *The Adventures of Huckleberry Finn* from three to five times during his academic career, and thus gain ever-expanding insights according to his state of readiness: a condensed version in elementary school; an abridged version in junior high; then in senior high school and undergraduate school, a definitive text, in each case using an approach consistent with the academic level. Bruner believes that through the spiral approach students could be profitably introduced to even so complex a concept as tragedy at a very early age.[16]

In selecting suitable literature for his students the teacher often confronts the thorny problem of satisfying community standards of morality and good taste—which in many cases may not be too enlightened, in the view of many teachers. Unfortunately, this problem does not submit readily to simple solution. It does not seem reasonable to state absolutely that teachers may teach anything and that students may

[13] Bruner, pp. 13–14.
[14] Perrine, *Story and Structure*, p. 364.
[15] *Ibid.*, p. 187.
[16] Bruner, pp. 52–53.

read anything. On the other hand, it is no more reasonable to require some of the inferior junior novels or *Peter Rabbit* as "safe" reading for intelligent secondary school students. Complicating the matter further is the fact that the traditions of local autonomy are deeply embedded in the American system of government, giving boards of education virtually complete power to develop their own curricula in accordance with particular community demands. Often, however, "community demands" may in reality reflect the will of but one person or a minority group. I have recently been told of an incident in which one parent in a moderate-sized community almost had *A Separate Peace* stricken from a reading list duly formulated by the faculty on the grounds that it contains the offensive word "damn." In speaking of *The Catcher in the Rye* Edward P. J. Corbett's comment applies appropriately here: "Granting the shock potential of such language. . . .to maintain that four letter words of themselves . . . can corrupt is another matter."[17]

All this does not mean to say that literature *per se* cannot corrupt or degrade. One knows too well that pornography and salacious literature can do substantial damage to some young minds. But the English teacher has on his side the fact that this type of literature is seldom if ever superior art, and on aesthetic grounds alone has little to commend it for classroom use. Yet even if one would argue, as has been argued here, that inferior art does have pedagogical value in serving to establish standards for comparison and contrast, the teacher would still be confronted with the problem of presenting the work to students who really are neither mature, intelligent, nor self-disciplined enough to profit from a frank study of such works. Finally, a work that some teachers would consider in bad taste, like James Baldwin's *Another Country* or Henry Miller's *Tropic of Capricorn*, can usually be handled quite well by the intelligent student on his own. Seldom do books of this nature require the help of a teacher. They are accessible and obvious to anyone who has been trained to read superior fiction like many of those covered here. In general, students should be permitted to read anything, provided that they are properly guided in their reading, and that they can respond to this guidance in such a way as to give substance and depth to their education. The sad fact is, however, that parents and teachers (it is the parents' responsibility as well as the teacher's) are sometimes ill-equipped to offer this guidance.

[17] Corbett, p. 441.

One must distinguish between an immoral novel and a novel that portrays immorality. Corbett observes that "Cardinal Newman once said that we cannot have a sinless literature about a sinful people."[18] Corbett continues on the same page: "No novel is immoral merely because vice is represented in it. Immorality creeps in as a result of the author's attitude toward the vice he is portraying and his manner of rendering the scene." A work like *The Catcher in the Rye* portrays immorality but is by no means an immoral novel, despite the fact that many well-intentioned people have branded it so. Often their judgment is based on the fact that it contains four-letter words which are unacceptable in polite speech. But, as Donald M. Fiene points out, "No amount of logic, no careful pointing out that Holden *himself* does not use the word, can ever persuade the shocked ones from their loathing and disgust."[19]

I assign *The Catcher in the Rye* in English methods courses as required reading, and find that after careful study most students become very fond of it, and are hopeful that they might some day have the good fortune to teach it. They tend to corroborate Granville Hicks' observation that students identify more closely with Holden than with characters like Jake Barnes, Augie March, and Jay Gatsby.[20] In fact, they are not so convinced as their instructor that Holden's greatest failing is his incapacity for charity. Rather, they are most favorably impressed with his perceptivity, idealism, and moral indignation.

It is hard to see how a work like *The Catcher in the Rye* can really corrupt a student. Neither Salinger nor Holden condones or justifies immorality in any way. There are no sexually provocative scenes or discussions. Indeed, Holden's attempt to consummate the sex act ends in disillusionment and fiasco. He becomes painfully aware that sex does not mean as much as the world of adults has made of it. In short, he gains an insight well worth sharing with other young people. In this sense the book actually promotes morality. To be sure, sex is discussed frankly and openly in this work. But as D. H. Lawrence points out, sex in art "does not function as sex functions outside art; it does not elicit

[18] *Ibid.*, p. 442.

[19] Donald M. Fiene, "From a Study of Salinger: Controversy in *The Catcher*," *The Realist*, I (December, 1961), p. 23.

[20] Granville Hicks, "J. D. Salinger: Search for Wisdom," *Saturday Review of Literature*, XLII (July 25, 1959), p. 13.

either our moral or our erotic response."[21] It is a virtue of art that through it taboo subjects are made more accessible for discussion, and from intelligent discussion comes understanding, which in turn provides a rational basis for desirable behavior.

The National Council of Teachers of English has in recent years become concerned over community attitudes toward the teaching of certain books in the schools. This concern is expressed in the following excerpt:

The censorship pressures that get the most publicity are those of small groups that protest the use of a limited number of books with realistic elements: *Huckleberry Finn, Brave New World,* 1984, *Grapes of Wrath* to name a few. Frequently the victims are among our best teachers who, encouraged by the excellent literature newly accessible to students in inexpensive paperbacks, have ventured outside the narrow boundaries of conventional textbooks.[22]

There can be little doubt that if our best teachers become "victims" of this kind of an attitude then all our students are being done a grave disservice. Nevertheless, even if teachers are not permitted to teach controversial works, this need not make it impossible, or even difficult for them to teach well, and to provide their students with a proper education. There are many superior works that are "safe": *Billy Budd, The Red Badge of Courage,* much of Faulkner, Dickens, and ever so many others. And, no teacher can be prevented from suggesting to parents certain books that merit reading, or from encouraging students to read on their own books that are available at a local library, but not included in the school curriculum.

The best resource that the teacher has at his disposal to help realize the lofty aims outlined in this chapter is his liberal education. But a liberal education needs constant replenishment and nourishment. Knowledge, like fish on a market shelf, needs replacement in time. Despite the fact that more needs to be done, much has been done to improve teacher education and to encourage able people to enter the profession. Salaries have improved, tax money has been committed in ever-increasing quantities to the needs of education (though recently there has been less expenditure of public money for education), and the

[21] D. H. Lawrence, *The Failure and Triumph of Art* (Evanston: Northwestern University Press, 1960), p. 144.
[22] *The Student's Right to Lead* (Champaign: NCTE, 1962), p. 10.

universities are more sensitive than they have ever been before to their stake in and their responsibilities to elementary and secondary education. Modern scholarship and the paperback-book industry have put resources unthought of a generation ago at the disposal of the teacher. Publishers like D. C. Heath, Harcourt-Brace, Wadsworth, Norton, and many others have commissioned scholars to compile case books and anthologies of pertinent criticism containing material that it would take many hours of labor to gather on one's own. The Allan Swallow Co. offers a unique service in its four-volume checklist of pertinent criticism of all major fiction and poetry in English and American literature, and the journals of the NCTE, *College English* and the *English Journal* in particular, contain critical and professional articles of immeasurable value to all teachers of English. In most major libraries throughout the country, a service is now available through the Educational Resources Information Center (ERIC) which provides lists of scholarly and interpretative articles on many specific works of literature. The bibliography of general and specific works appearing at the end of this book should also prove of value to the teacher.

Bibliography

Bibliographical entries with asterisks appear both in anthologies of criticism as well as in scholarly journals or books. In this bibliography these entries are listed as items appearing in journals and books. But in the footnotes of the text they are listed as items appearing in anthologies of criticism, thus providing the reader with a double reference.

*Adams, Richard P. "The Unity and Coherence of *Huckleberry Finn*," *Tulane Studies in English*, VI (1956), 87–103.

Aiken, Conrad. "Silent Snow, Secret Snow," in *Reading Modern Short Stories*, ed. Jarvis A. Thurston, pp. 349–364.

Aldridge, John W. (ed.) *Critiques and Essays in Modern Fiction*, 1920–1951. New York: The Ronald Press Co., 1952.

Anderson, Sherwood. *Winesburg, Ohio*. New York: The Viking Press, Inc., 1964.

Aristotle. "Poetics," in *Aristotle's Theory of Poetry and Fine Art*, ed. S. H. Butcher.

Arvin, Newton. *Herman Melville: A Critical Biography*. New York: William Sloane Associates, 1950.

Baldwin, James. *Notes of a Native Son*. Boston: Beacon Press, 1957.

Bellow, Saul. *The Adventures of Augie March*. New York: Viking Press, 1964.

————. "Deep Readers of the World, Beware!" *New York Times Book Review*. February 15, 1959, 1, 43.

Bergson, Henry. "Laughter," in *Comedy*, ed. Wylie Sypher.

Bloom, Lynn., *et al. Bear, Man, and God*. New York: Random House, Inc. 1963.

Blotner, Joseph L. and Gwynn, Frederick L. *The Fiction of J. D. Salinger*. Pittsburgh: The University of Pittsburgh Press, 1958.

Booth, Wayne C. *The Rhetoric of Fiction*. Chicago: The University of Chicago Press, 1965.

Bowden, Edwin T. *The Dungeon of the Heart*. New York: The Macmillan Co., 1961.

Bowen, Robert O. "The Salinger Syndrome: Charity Against Whom?" *Ramparts*, I (May, 1962), 52–60.

Bradley, A. C. "Hegel's Theory of Tragedy," in Anne and Henry Paolucci, eds., *Hegel on Tragedy.*

Bradley, Scully, *et al.* (eds.) *The Adventures of Huckleberry Finn*, by Mark Twain. New York: W. W. Norton & Co., Inc., 1962.

————. *The Red Badge of Courage*, by Stephen Crane. New York: W. W. Norton & Co., Inc., 1962.

Branch, Edgar. "Mark Twain and J. D. Salinger: A Study in Literary Continuity," *American Quarterly*, IX (Summer, 1957), 144–158.

Braswell, William. "Melville's *Billy Budd* as an Inside Narrative," *American Literature*, XXIX (May, 1957), 133–146.

Brooks, Cleanth. *The Well-Wrought Urn.* New York: Harcourt, Brace & World, Inc., 1947.

Brown, Leonard (ed.) *A Quarto of Modern Literature.* New York: Charles Scribner's Sons, 1964.

Bruner, Jerome S. *The Process of Education.* New York: Alfred A. Knopf, Inc., 1960.

Burton, Dwight L. *Literature Study in the High Schools.* New York: Holt, Rinehart and Winston, Inc., 1964.

Butcher, S. H. *Aristotle's Theory of Poetry and Fine Art.* New York: Dover Publications, Inc., 1951.

Capote, Truman. *Other Voices, Other Rooms.* New York: Alfred A. Knopf, Inc., 1948.

Caspar, Leonard. "The Case Against Captain Vere," *Perspective*, V (Summer, 1952), 146–152.

Cather, Willa. "Paul's Case," in *Five Stories.* New York: Alfred A. Knopf, Inc., 1958.

Chase, Richard. *Herman Melville: A Critical Study.* New York: The Macmillan Co., 1949.

Clemens, Samuel Langhorne. *The Adventures of Huckleberry Finn.* New York: New American Library of World Literature, Inc., 1964.

Cohen, B. Bernard. *Writing about Literature.* Chicago: Scott, Foresman and Co., 1963.

Corbett, Edward P. J. "Raise High the Barriers, Censors," *America,* CIV (January 7, 1961), 441–444.

Costello, Donald P. "The Language of *The Catcher in the Rye*," *American Speech*, XXXIV (October, 1959), 172–181.

*Cowley, Malcolm. "A Natural History of American Naturalism." *Kenyon Review*, IX (Summer, 1947), 414–435.

*Cox, James Trammel. "The Imagery of *The Red Badge of Courage*," *Modern Fiction Studies*, V (Autumn, 1959), 209–219.

Cox, Kenyon. *The Classic Point of View.* New York: Charles Scribner's Sons, 1911.

Crane, Stephen. *The Red Badge of Courage*, ed. Richard Chase. Boston: Houghton Mifflin Co., 1960.

Daiches, David. *A Study of Literature for Readers and Critics*. Ithaca: Cornell University Press, 1948.

*De Voto, Bernard. *Mark Twain's America*. Boston: Houghton Mifflin Co., 1932.

Dewey, John. *Art as Experience*. New York: G. P. Putnam's Sons, 1958.

Dreiser, Theodore. *An American Tragedy*. Cleveland: World Publishing Co., 1962.

*Eliot, T. S. "Introduction," *The Adventures of Huckleberry Finn*, by Mark Twain. London: The Cresset Press, 1950.

Ellison, Ralph. "The Negro Writer in America," *Partisan Review*, XXV (Spring, 1958), 212–222.

Emerson, Ralph Waldo. "The American Scholar," "Fate," "Nature," and "Self-Reliance," in Norman Foerster (ed.), *American Poetry and Prose*, 461–523.

Farrell, James T. *Studs Lonigan*. New York: Vanguard Press, Inc., 1960.

Faulkner, William. "Barn Burning," in Albert Erskine and Robert Penn Warren (eds.), *Short Story Masterpieces*. New York: Dell Publishing Co., Inc., 1954), 162–182.

———. *The Bear*, in Norman Foerster (ed.), *American Poetry and Prose*, 1530–83.

———. *Intruder in the Dust*. New York: Modern Library, Inc., 1948.

Fiedler, Leslie. *An End to Innocence*. Boston: Beacon Press, 1955.

Fiene, Donald M. "From a Study of Salinger: Controversy in *The Catcher*," *The Realist*, I (December, 1961), 23–25.

Fitzgerald, F. Scott. *This Side of Paradise*. New York: Dell Publishing Co., Inc., 1948.

Foerster, Norman (ed.) *American Poetry and Prose*. Boston: Houghton Mifflin Co., 1962.

Fogle, Richard Harter. "*Billy Budd*—Acceptance or Irony," *Tulane Studies in English*, VIII (1958), 109–113.

Forster, E. M. *Aspects of the Novel*. New York: Harcourt, Brace & World, Inc., 1954.

Gassner, John. "Aristotelian Literary Criticism," in S. H. Butcher (ed.), *Aristotle's Theory of Poetry and Fine Art*.

Glick, Wendell. "Expediency and Absolute Morality in *Billy Budd*," *Publications of the Modern Language Association*, LXVIII (March, 1953), 103–110.

Gordon, Edward J. "Levels of Teaching and Testing," *English Journal*, XLIV (September, 1955), 330–334, 342.

*Greenfield, Stanley B. "The Unmistakable Stephen Crane," *Publications of the Modern Language Association*, LXXIII (December, 1958), 562–572.

*Gullason, Thomas Arthur. "The Fatal Ending of *Huckleberry Finn*," *American Literature*, XXIX (March, 1957), 86–91.

Guth, Hans P. *English Today and Tomorrow*. Englewood Cliffs: Prentice-Hall, Inc., 1964.

Hamm, Victor M. *The Pattern of Criticism*. Milwaukee: The Bruce Publishing Co., 1951.

*Hart, John E. "*The Red Badge of Courage* as Myth and Symbol," *University of Kansas City Review*, XIX (Summer, 1953), 249–256.

Hartwick, Harry. *The Foreground of American Fiction*. New York: The American Book Co., 1934.

Hassan, Ihab H. "Rare Quixotic Gesture: The Fiction of J. D. Salinger," *The Western Review*, XXI (Summer, 1957), 261–280.

Hawthorne, Nathaniel. "My Kinsman, Major Molineux," in Norman Foerster, (ed.), *American Poetry and Prose*, 608–618.

Hayakawa, S. I. *Language in Thought and Action*. New York: Harcourt, Brace & World Inc., 1964.

Heiserman, Arthur and Miller, James E., Jr. "J. D. Salinger: Some Crazy Cliff," *Western Humanities Review*, X (Spring, 1956), 129–137.

Hemingway, Ernest. *A Farewell to Arms*. New York: Charles Scribner's Sons, 1957.

———. *For Whom the Bell Tolls*. New York: Charles Scribner's Sons, 1956.

———. "Indian Camp," "The Battler," and "Big Two-Hearted River," in *In Our Time*. New York: Charles Scribner's Sons, 1958.

———. "Fathers and Sons," "The Killers," and "A Way You'll Never Be," in *The Snows of Kilimanjaro and Other Stories*. New York: Charles Scribner's Sons, 1961. *The Sun Also Rises*. New York: Charles Scribner's Sons,

———. *The Sun Also Rises*. New York: Charles Scribner's Sons, 1954.

Henry, George H. "Method: The New Home of the Liberal Spirit," in Dwight. L. Burton (ed.), *English Education Today*. Champaign: National Council of Teachers of English, 1963, 19–23.

Hicks, Granville. "J. D. Salinger: Search for Wisdom," *Saturday Review*, XLII (July 25, 1959), 13, 30.

Hillocks, George, Jr. "The Theme-Concept Unit in Literature." *Patterns and Models for Teaching English*. Champaign: National Council of Teachers of English, 1964, 17–25.

Hoffman, Daniel G. *Form and Fable in American Fiction*. New York: Oxford University Press, 1961.

Hoffman, Frederick J. *The Modern Novel in America*. Chicago: Henry Regnery Co., 1951.

Hofstadter, Richard. *Anti-Intellectualism in American Life*. New York: Alfred A. Knopf, Inc., 1963.

Hook, J. N. *The Teaching of Hifgh School English.* New York: The Ronald Press Co., 1965.

Hulme, T. E. "Romanticism and Classicism," in R. W. Stallman (ed.), *Critiques and Essays in Criticism*, 1920-1948, 3–16.

James, Henry. *The Art of Fiction and Other Essays.* New York: Oxford University Press, 1948.

Kerouac, Jack. *On the Road.* New York: The Viking Press, Inc., 1957.

Knowles, John. *A Separate Peace.* New York: Dell Publishing Co., Inc., 1965.

Krutch, Joseph Wood. *The Modern Temper.* New York: Harcourt, Brace & World, Inc., 1956.

———. "Speaking of Books," *New York Times Book Review*, May 23, 1954, 2.

*Lane, Lauriat, Jr. "Why *Huckleberry Finn* is a Great World Novel," *College English*, XVII (Oc ober, 1955), 1–5.

Lawrence, D. H. *The Failure and Triumph of Art.* Evans on: Northwestern University Press, 1960.

Lewis, John S. and Sisk, Jean C. *Teaching English*, 7–12. New York: American Book Co., 1963.

Lewis, R. W. B. *The American Adam.* Chicago: The Universi y of Chicago Press, 1955.

Light, James F. "Salinger's *The Catcher in the Rye*," *The Explicator*, XVIII (June, 1960), 59.

Loban, Walter, *et al. Teaching Language and Literature, Grades* 7–12. New York: Harcourt, Brace & World, Inc., 1961.

London, Jack. *Martin Eden.* New York: Rinehart and Co., Inc., 1956.

*Lubbock, Percy. *The Craft of Fiction.* New York: Charles Scribner's, Sons, 1929.

*Marcus, Erin and Mordecai. "Animal Imagery in *The Red Badge of Courage*," *Modern Language Notes*, LXXIV (February, 1959), 108–111.

*Marx, Leo. "Mr. Eliot, Mr. Trilling, and *Huckleberry Finn*," *The American Scholar*, XXII (Autumn, 1953), 423–440.

Mead, Margaret. *Coming of Age in Samoa.* New York: New American Library of World Literature, Inc., 1936.

Melville, Herman. *Billy Budd*, in Norman Foerster (ed.), *American Poetry and Prose*, 723–762.

———. *Moby Dick.* New York: The Bobbs-Merrill Co., Inc., 1964.

———. *Redburn.* Garden City: Doubleday & Co., Inc., 1957.

Mencken, H. L. *A Book of Prefaces.* New York: Alfred A. Knopf, Inc., 1917.

Meredith, George. "An Essay on Comedy," in Wylie Sypher (ed.), *Comedy*

Miller, Arthur. "Tragedy and the Common Man," in Leonard Brown (ed.), *A Quarto of Modern Literature.*

Mumford, Lewis. *Herman Melville.* New York: Harcourt, Brace and Co., 1967.

Murry, John Middleton. "Herman Melville's Silence," *Times Literary Supplement* (London), July 10, 1924, 433.

Oldsey, Bernard S. "The Movies in the Rye," *College English*, XXIII (December, 1961), 209–215.

Paolucci, Anne and Henry (eds.) *Hegel on Tragedy.* Garden City: Doubleday & Co., Inc., 1962.

Perrine, Laurence. *Sound and Sense.* New York: Harcourt, Brace & World, Inc., 1963.

———. *Story and Structure.* New York: Harcourt, Brace & World, Inc., 1959.

*Pritchett, V. S. "*Huckleberry Finn* and the Cruelty of American Humor," *New Statesman and Nation* (London), August 2, 1941, 13.

*Rahv. Philip. *Image and Idea.* New York: New Directions, 1949.

*———. "The Symbolic Fallacy in Crane Criticism," *Kenyon Review*, XVIII (Spring, 1956), 276–287.

Riesman, David, *et al. The Lonely Crowd.* New York: Doubleday & Co., Inc., 1955.

Salinger, J. D. *The Catcher in the Rye.* New York: Bantam Books, Inc., 1964.

Sampson, George. *English for the English.* London: Cambridge University Press, 1921.

Schorer, Mark. *The Story: A Critical Anthology.* Englewood Cliffs: Prentice-Hall, Inc., 1950.

*———. "Technique as Discovery," *Hudson Review*, I (Spring, 1948), 67–87.

*Schroeder, John W. "Stephen Crane Embattled," *University of Kansas City Review*, XVII (Winter, 1950), 123–129.

Simonson, Harold P. and Hager, Philip E. (eds.) *Salinger's Catcher in the Rye, Clamor vs. Criticism.* Boston: D. C. Heath and Co., 1963.

Stafford, William T. (ed.) *Billy Budd and the Critics.* Belmont: Wadsworth Publishing Co., 1964.

Stallman, Robert Wooster (ed.) *Critiques and Essays in Criticism, 1920–1948.* New York: The Ronald Press Co., 1949.

*———. "Notes Toward an Analysis of *The Red Badge of Courage*," in *The Red Badge of Courage*, by Stephen Crane. New York: Random House, Inc., 1951.

*———. "The Scholar's Net: Literary Sources," *College English*, XVII (October, 1955), 20–22.

Steinbeck, John. *The Red Pony,* in *The Portable Steinbeck.* New York: The Viking Press, Inc., 1963.

Stern, Milton R. *The Fine-Hammered Steel of Herman Melville.* Urbana: The University of Illinois Press, 1957.

Stevenson, David L. "The Activists," *Daedalus* (Spring, 1963), 238–249.

Stone, George Winchester (ed.) *Issues, Problems, and Approaches in the Teaching of English.* New York: Holt, Rinehart and Winston, Inc., 1963.

Student's Right to Read, The. Champaign: National Council of Teachers of English, 1962.

Sypher, Wylie. *Comedy.* Garden City: Doubleday & Co., Inc., 1956.

Thompson, Lawrence. *Melville's Quarrel with God.* Princeton: Princeton University Press, 1952.

Thoreau, Henry David. "Civil Disobedience" and *Walden,* ed. Sherman Paul. Boston: Houghton Mifflin Co., 1960.

Thurston, Jarvis A. (ed.) *Reading Modern Short Stories.* Chicago: Scott, Foresman and Co., 1955.

Tindall, William York. "The Ceremony of Innocence," in R. M. McIver (ed), *Great Moral Dilemmas in Literature, Past and Present.* New York: Harper & Brothers, 1956.

*Trilling, Lionel. "The Greatness of *Huck Finn," The Liberal Imagination.* New York: The Viking Press, Inc., 1950.

————. "Of This Time, Of That Place," in Jarvis A. Thurston, *Reading Modern Short Stories,* 451–485.

Vales, Robert L. "Thief and Theft in *Huckleberry Finn," American Literature,* XXXVII (January, 1966), 420–429.

*Walcutt, Charles C. *American Literary Naturalism: A Divided Stream.* Minneapolis: The University of Minnesota Press, 1956.

*Warren, Robert Penn. "Hemingway," *Kenyon Review,* IX (Winter, 1947), 1–28.

Watson, E. L. Grant. "Melville's Testament of Acceptance," *New England Quarterly,* VI (June, 1933), 319–327.

Weaver, Raymond M. *Herman Melville, Mariner and Mystic.* New York: Pageant Books, Inc., 1960.

————. *The Shorter Novels of Herman Melville.* New York: Liveright Publishing Corp., 1928.

West, Ray B., Jr. "The Unity of *Billy Budd," Hudson Review,* V (Spring, 1952), 120–127.

Wilder, Thornton. *Three Plays.* New York: Bantam Books, Inc., 1961.

Witham, W. Tasker. *The Adolescent in the American Novel, 1920–1960.* New York: Frederick Ungar Publishing Co., 1964.

Withim, Phil. "*Billy Budd:* The Testament of Resistance," *Modern Language Quarterly,* XX (June, 1959), 115–127.

Wolfe, Thomas. *Look Homeward, Angel.* New York: Charles Scribner's Sons, 1952.

*Wyndham, George. "A Remarkable Book," *The London New Review*, XIV (January, 1896), 30–40.

Zola, Emile. *The Experimental Novel and Other Essays*. New York: Haskell House, 1964.

Index of fictional works

Adventures of Augie March, The, 36

Adventures of Huckleberry Finn, The, 2, 6, 19, 21, 23, 34, 41, 44, 47, 75–76, 85, 91, 93, 105, 112, 114, 129–130, 134–135, 142, 145, 147–148, 151, 156, 159

American Tragedy, An, 33, 103, 105, 116, 134, 149

"Barn Burning," 37, 47, 101

"Bear, The," 41, 86, 100, 118

Billy Budd, 30, 78–79, 83, 89, 94, 96, 105, 116, 126, 129, 132, 134–135, 144, 148–149, 159

Catcher in the Rye, The, 23–24, 32, 39, 77, 98, 100, 115, 133, 142, 149, 157–158

Intruder in the Dust, 40–41, 86, 101, 105, 151

Look Homeward Angel, 11, 42, 59, 86, 117

Martin Eden, 36, 86, 105, 118

"My Kinsman, Major Molineux," 41, 151

"Of This Time, Of That Place," 32

On the Road, 40, 62, 102, 151

Other Voices, Other Rooms, 39–40, 85, 151

"Paul's Case," 38, 85, 144

Red Badge of Courage, The, 28, 47, 54–55, 77–79, 82–83, 89, 97–98, 114, 135, 147–149, 159

Redburn, 41, 60, 95

Red Pony, The, 37, 87

Separate Peace, A, 43, 65, 86, 101, 118, 150

"Silent Snow, Secret Snow," 39, 85

Studs Lonigan, 36, 117, 134

This Side of Paradise, 12, 42, 118, 151

Winesburg, Ohio, 26, 43–44, 60, 86, 149

Index of principal fictional characters

Amory Blaine, 12, 42, 118, 152

Augie March, 36–37, 62, 158

Billy Budd, 30–32, 37, 47, 57, 65, 79–81, 83–84, 94–98, 103, 116, 126–128, 148

Chick Mallison, 40–41, 101

Claggart, 30–32, 37, 42, 79–80, 94–97, 126

Clyde Griffiths, 24, 33–35, 53, 61–62, 65, 103–104, 117–118, 123–124, 128, 150–151

Gene Forrester, 43–44, 65, 86, 101–102, 118, 134, 150

Gene Gant, 42–44, 59, 65, 86, 117–118

George Willard, 43, 60–61, 65, 86, 149

Henry Fleming, 28–30, 44, 47, 54–59, 63, 65, 78, 79, 97–98, 103, 114–115, 135, 147–148

Holden Caulfield, 23–29, 39, 43–44, 47, 55–57, 62, 65–66, 77, 79, 81–82, 86, 99–100, 102, 115, 133–135, 138, 142, 149, 158

Huck Finn, 19–22, 24, 27–29, 33–34, 39, 41, 43–44, 47, 52–57, 59, 61, 65, 75–76, 81, 91–93, 99–100, 103, 106, 112–113, 133–134, 138, 146

Ike McCaslin, 41, 43, 58-59, 61, 65, 79, 86, 100–101, 103, 106, 118, 134

Jody, 37, 87

Joel Knox, 39, 151

Martin Eden, 36–37, 65, 86, 102–103, 118–119, 134

Nick Adams, 38, 42, 63–65, 79, 144

Paul, 38–39, 47, 85, 134

Redburn, 42, 60, 63, 104

Robin, 41–42, 60, 104–105, 130, 151

Sal Paradise, 40, 53, 62, 102

Sarty Snopes, 37, 47, 101, 134

Studs Lonigan, 34–37, 61, 65, 117, 123, 128, 134–135

Tertan, 32

Vere, 30–34, 47, 57, 65, 80, 84, 94, 96–97, 126–128, 148

Index of principal fictional characters